Contents

What do you think of this book? We want to hear from you!

Microsoft is interested in hearing your feedback so we can continually improve our books and learning resources for you. To participate in a brief online survey, please visit:

www.microsoft.com/learning/booksurvey/

Chapter 6
Modifying Your Web Browser — 85

Chapter 7
Fixing the Broken Blocks — 125

Chapter 8
Managing the Data — 141

Chapter 9
Building Your Own Weather Tracker Application — 187

Introduction

Microsoft Visual Basic 2008 Express Edition (and the other Visual Studio 2008 Express Edition products) is, in my opinion, one of the best and most intelligent ideas to come from the Developer Division at Microsoft. I'm applauding and cheering for the people who had this brilliant idea because I believe there is a real need and demand for a world-class, powerful product for hobbyist programmers, students, and professional developers. And Visual Basic 2008 Express Edition provides all of that and more.

Visual Basic 2008 Express Edition is a fully functional subset of Visual Studio 2008, suitable for creating and maintaining Windows applications and libraries. It's not a timed-bomb edition, a demo, or a feature-limited version—no, it's a key Microsoft initiative to reach more people and give them the ability to have fun while creating cool software.

Who Is This Book For?

This book is for everybody: students, hobbyist pro-grammers, and people who always thought programming was a tough task. It's for people who have ideas like "I wish I could build a tool to store all my recipes and then print them and send them to my friends," "I wish I could build this cool card game that I have never found elsewhere," "I wish I could build this cool software to store my DVD and CD collection," "I wish I could build this software to help me work with matrices and plot graphics for my math class," and many more projects that you can imagine!

This book is for people who have ideas but don't know how to bring them to reality. And it's a good introduction to the art and science of developing software.

How This Book Is Organized

This book consists of nine chapters, each covering a particular feature or technology about Visual Basic 2008 Express Edition. Most chapters build on previous chapters, so you should plan on reading the material sequentially.

Conventions and Features in This Book

This book presents information using conventions designed to make the information readable and easy to follow. Before you start the book, read the following list, which explains conventions you'll see throughout the book and points out helpful features in the book that you might want to use:

- Each exercise is a series of tasks. Each task is presented as a series of numbered steps (step 1, 2, and so on). Each exercise is preceded by a procedural heading that lets you know what you will accomplish in the exercise.

- Boxes labeled *TIP*, *NOTE*, *MORE INFO*, and so on, provide additional information or alternative methods for completing a step successfully.

- Boxes labeled *CAUTION* alert you to information you need to verify before continuing.

- Text that you type appears in bold.

- Menu commands, dialog box titles, and other user interface elements appear with each word capitalized, such as in "click Save As."

- A plus sign (+) between two key names means that you must press those keys at the same time. For example, "Press Alt+Tab" means that you hold down the Alt key while you press the Tab key.

- Code listings appear in a monospaced font in this book.

- Sidebars throughout the book provide more in-depth information about the content. The sidebars might contain background information, design tips, or features related to the information being discussed.

- Each chapter ends with an "In Summary..." section that briefly reviews what you learned in the current chapter and previews what the next chapter will present.

System Requirements

You'll need the following hardware and software to complete the exercises in this book:

- Windows Vista, Microsoft Windows XP with Service Pack 2, or Microsoft Windows Server 2003 with Service Pack 2

- Visual Basic 2008 Express Edition

- 1 GHz 32-bit (x86) processor

- 1 GB MB RAM (512 MB minimum)

- 40 GB hard drive with at least 15 GB of available space

- Support for Super VGA graphics (for support for DirectX 9 graphics, see the recommended requirements at *www.microsoft.com/windows/products/windowsvista/editions/systemrequirements.mspx*)

- CD-ROM or DVD-ROM drive

- Microsoft mouse or compatible pointing device

You'll also need administrator access to your computer to configure SQL Server 2005 Express Edition.

> **NOTE**
> The companion DVD contains the Visual Basic 2008 Express Edition software needed to complete the exercises in this book. The DVD also includes the other Visual Studio 2008 Express Editions—for Visual C#, Visual C++, and Web development. You can install any of the Express Edition products included on the DVD. See Chapter 2, "Installing Visual Basic 2008 Express Edition," for detailed installation instructions.

Code Samples

You can download the code samples for the examples in this book from the book's companion content page at the following address: *http://www.microsoft.com/mspress/companion/9780735625419/*. You'll use the code samples and starter solutions as you perform the exercises in the book. By using the code samples, you won't waste time creating files that aren't relevant to the exercise. The files and step-by-step instructions also let you learn by doing, which is an effective way to acquire and remember new skills. You'll also find the complete solutions if you want to verify your work or simply want to look at them.

Installing the Code Samples

Follow these steps to install the code samples on your computer.

1. Download the code samples from *http://www.microsoft.com/mspress/companion/9780735625419/.*

2. After you download the code samples file, run the installer.

3. Follow the instructions that appear.

   The code samples are installed in the Documents\Microsoft Press\VB 2008 Express folder on your computer.

Using the Code Samples

Each chapter in this book explains when and how to use any code samples for that chapter. When it's time to use a code sample, the book will list the instructions for how to open the files. The chapters are built around scenarios that simulate real programming projects so you can easily apply the skills you learn to your own work.

For those of you who like to know all the details, a list of the code sample projects appears in the following table. Almost all projects have solutions available for the practice exercises. The solutions for each project are included in the folder for each chapter and are labeled "Complete."

Project	Description
Chapters 1 and 2	No sample projects.
Chapter 3 MyFirstConsoleApplication	Application that takes two numbers, adds them together, and then displays the sum in a console window.
MyFirstWindowsApplication	Same application as MyFirstConsoleApplication, but this one displays the result in a message box.
Chapter 4 MyOwnBrowser	Simple Web browser application that enables the user to browse on the Internet.
Chapter 5 TestProject	Application that teaches you to use the most important features in Visual Basic 2008 Express Edition.
Chapter 6 MyOwnBrowser	This is the same application you developed in Chapter 4, enhanced with additional features. You'll add menus, toolbars, status and progress bars, and a navigation window with autocomplete. You'll also build a simple browser using Windows Presentation Foundation (WPF).

Project	Description
Chapter 7 Debugger	An application full of problems to help you learn how to debug an application by using features of Visual Basic 2008 Express Edition.
Chapter 8 CarTracker	An application enabling the user to track car ads from the Internet using a SQL Server 2005 Express database to store the information. You'll also be introduced to Language Integrated Query (LINQ).
Chapter 9 Weather Tracker	An application that runs in the system tray and has a nice user interface to display weather data collected by your application from the MSN Weather service. You'll also create a deployment package for the distribution of your application.

Uninstalling the Code Samples

Follow these steps to remove the code samples from your computer.

ON WINDOWS VISTA

1. In Control Panel, click Programs.
2. Under Programs and Features, click Uninstall a Program.
3. In the list of programs, select Microsoft Visual Basic 2008 Express Edition: Build a Program Now!, and then click Uninstall.
4. Follow the instructions on the screen to remove the code samples.

ON WINDOWS XP

1. In Control Panel, open Add or Remove Programs.

2. From the Currently Installed Programs list, select Microsoft Visual Basic 2008 Express Edition: Build a Program Now!, and click Remove.
3. Follow the instructions on the screen to remove the code samples.

Prerelease Software

This book was reviewed and tested against the November 2007 release candidate for Visual Studio 2008. This book is expected to be fully compatible with the final release of Visual Studio 2008. If there are any changes or corrections for this book, they'll be collected and added to a Microsoft Knowledge Base article. See the "Support for This Book" section later in this introduction for more information.

Technology Updates

As technologies related to this book are updated, links to additional information will be added to the Microsoft

Press Technology Updates Web page (*http://www.micro-soft.com/mspress/updates/*). Visit this page periodically for updates on Visual Studio 2008 and other technologies.

Support for This Book

Every effort has been made to ensure the accuracy of this book and the companion content. As corrections or changes are collected, they'll be added to a Microsoft Knowledge Base article. To view the list of known corrections for this book, visit *http://support.microsoft.com/*, and in the Search box, enter the book title.

Microsoft Press provides support for books and companion content at *http://www.microsoft.com/learning/support/books/*.

Questions and Comments

If you have comments, questions, or ideas regarding the book or the companion content or have questions that are not answered by visiting the sites listed earlier, please send them to Microsoft Press via e-mail to *mspinput@microsoft.com*.

Or you can send them via postal mail to the following address:

Microsoft Press
Attn: Visual Basic 2008 Express Edition: Build a Program Now! Editor
One Microsoft Way
Redmond, WA 98052-6399

Please note that Microsoft offers no software product support through these addresses.

About the Author

Patrice Pelland is a development manager at Microsoft working in the Online Services Group. He has a passion for Web 2.0 technologies, Silverlight, WCF, and ASP.NET. For the past four years, he has been working, teaching, evangelizing, and talking about these technologies to everyone.

For the past 14 years, he has been working in software development in various roles: developer, project lead, manager and mentor, and software engineer in QA organizations. He has vast experience spanning multiple technologies and fields, including Web development, developer tools, fiber optics telecommunication, aviation, and coffee and dairy companies. He also spent three years teaching computer science and software development at a college in Canada.

When not developing great tools for developers and helping customers throughout the world, he enjoys spending time with his family and friends, playing games on Xbox 360 and his PC, reading books, reading about cars, playing hockey, watching NHL hockey and NFL football, and having great dinners with good food and fine drinks with friends and family. He resides with his family in Sammamish, Washington.

Dedication

This book is dedicated to my family. My wife, Hélène, is my strength; because of her love and her respect, I am a better human being. She's beautiful—my idol, my inspiration, my sunshine, my best friend, my love, and an awesome mother! *Mon amour*, thanks for being who you are and for being there for me. I love you! Thanks to her for letting me repeat this crazy adventure of writing a book.

Thanks

First of all, thanks to my parents. Mom and Dad, you gave me all the chances to be what I am in life and you gave me the values to be the man I am. Thanks, and I love you!

A book is a huge adventure in somebody's life (imagine two ☺), and it would not be possible without the help of many people. I've always read the "thank you" sections in other people's books, and I was always amazed at how many people are needed to make a book what it is. Now I really understand why!

Although writing a book is tough—real tough—it's really satisfying at the same time. During the writing process, you sometimes have doubts, and I had my share of them, especially those nights at 3 a.m. when all other souls in the house were asleep, even my dog; when I was in front of my laptop with an exception and a white page in Microsoft Word. I can't remember how many times I said to my friends, "No, I won't be able to be there. I need to work on my book." But it's an awesome experience to write a book; everybody who has the chance should take the challenge!

That said, I first need to thank my lovely family for letting me do this to them again. My kids (Laura, 13, and Antoine, 11) and my wife, Hélène, were so great and *patient*. This time they said, "You're writing another book! Oh, no...we'll see you after Thanksgiving." But at the same time, they were respecting the space I needed and the time alone! You guys are great, and I love you!

I have to thank all the people at Microsoft Learning and the publishing team. I would especially like to thank Ben Ryan for offering me the chance to work with him again; Sandra for her constant motivation, help, and suggestions and also for helping me through all the hurdles of writing a book; and all the folks on the publishing team for all their help getting the job done and producing a real, tangible product. You guys have my respect for working day in, day out in the crazy world of publishing.

I would also like to thank all the people in the Visual Basic, C#, Windows Forms, MSDN, and setup teams who helped me by answering all my questions in a dynamic and constantly changing product life cycle. I would like to thank more specifically Dan Fernandez, Joe Binder, Brian Keller, Brian Johnson, Hong Gao, Jay Roxe, Kavitha Radhakrishnan, Kent Sharkey, Lisa Feigenbaum, Shamez Rajan, Steve Lasker, Aaron Stebner, and Habib Heydarian.

Thanks also to my colleagues at MSN for always giving me good words of encouragement and to my friends Pascal, Simon, Nicolas, John, and Patrice for reviewing the samples and some chapters.

Thanks to my good friends here in the Puget Sound area for the kind words of encouragement and to my family and friends in Canada for understanding why I'm not calling or giving any news. Sorry, Mom and Dad!

Thanks to everybody I might have forgotten!

Patrice Pelland
November 2007
Sammamish, WA

Chapter 1
Introducing Microsoft Visual Basic 2008 Express Edition

Maybe you've decided to try programming and find yourself with this book. If that's the case, you've come to the right place. This book is all about introducing you to the art, science, and joys of creating software for Microsoft Windows—yes, the same Microsoft Windows you probably use every day. Throughout the book, I'll show you how to build applications that are similar to many of the applications you use on a regular basis, such as your Internet browser, your word processor, your e-mail software, and your personal finance application. You're probably wondering how you could possibly do this with no programming experience. Don't worry. By the time you finish this book, you'll be a believer. We'll have a blast, and because you'll actually be building applications as you follow along with each exercise, you'll see for yourself just how easy it can be.

What is this .NET thing everybody is talking about? Maybe you've seen the term somewhere online or have come across it in the jobs section of your Sunday newspaper. A good analogy is that .NET—also called the .NET Framework—is to a software developer what tools and manuals are to an auto mechanic.

Here is a formal definition of the .NET Framework:

The .NET Framework is a platform with which you can develop software applications and libraries called managed applications; it provides you with the compiler and tools you need to build, debug, and execute managed applications.

For our purposes, you could say that .NET is the platform that gives you everything you need to develop and run managed applications that run on Windows.

We say that applications are *managed* because their execution is managed by the .NET Framework. In fact, the .NET Framework manages the execution by providing a controlled runtime environment that offers a wide variety of services, such as loading your applications, managing memory, and monitoring and maintaining security and integrity while the application runs. Before .NET (and Java), applications were unmanaged because they were not executed by a controlled runtime environment. No other component of the operating system provides the services .NET offers. The applications had to manage their own services, which sometimes led to erroneous code, security holes, and data corruption. Because of these problems, applications were tough to maintain and debug.

NOTE
Throughout this book, I'll use the terms *framework* and *.NET Framework* synonymously.

The .NET Framework provides you with a wide variety of tools, such as compilers, debuggers, programming languages, an execution engine (named the Common Language Runtime [CLR]), developer tools, and a large number of predefined "building block" libraries. These libraries are named Framework Class Libraries (FCLs). You can think of each .NET component as a building block in a house and each version of .NET as an insulation layer in the walls of a house. Figure 1-1 illustrates how many versions of .NET are on the market, as well as what components have been added and in which version they belong.

Visual Studio 2008

NET 3.5

NET 3.0

NET 2.0

CLR
WinForms
Web Services
ASP.NET

WCF

WF

WPF

CardSpace

LINQ

AJAX

REST

Figure 1-1
Additive versions of the .NET Framework

NOTE

What do the other abbreviations and names in Figure 1-1 mean? WF is the Windows Workflow Foundation, another building block that developers can use to help automate business processes through programs. CardSpace is a technology related to managing online identities—something like using a credit card. AJAX (Asynchronous JavaScript And XML) is used to develop Web applications, and REST (Representational State Transfer) is a programming architecture used for transferring data on the Web.

Some of these building blocks ship with the Windows Vista operating system. Two popular ones are Windows Presentation Foundation (WPF) and Windows Communication Foundation (WCF). WPF is a library that helps you build richer user interfaces and Windows Vista–like applications for Windows. WCF, as its name implies, is a library that helps two applications talk to each other using messages. To understand the relationship between .NET 3.0 and .NET 3.5, remember that .NET 3.0 comes with Windows Vista and .NET 3.5 comes with Visual Studio 2008. Language Integrated Query (LINQ), which simplifies writing code that manipulates data from various data sources (SQL Server databases, XML files, and so on), is one of the features in .NET 3.5 that we'll cover in this book.

IMPORTANT

It's not necessary to have Visual Studio to develop .NET applications, but using it offers many advantages, as you'll see in this book.

IMPORTANT

The CLR hasn't changed in Windows Vista and Visual Studio 2008; the CLR that is running on all operating systems is .NET 2.0.

I won't put you to sleep with all the definitions for each building block. We're going to use or talk about most of them in our projects in this book, and I'll introduce the blocks when appropriate. Just consider Figure 1-1 and return to it when you need to do so.

Two notes about this figure are worth mentioning.

First, look at the blue component on top of the concentric circles. Microsoft Visual Studio 2008 is not part of the .NET Framework, but it touches the .NET Framework at all levels. With Visual Studio 2008, you can develop applications that take advantage of all the components of the .NET Framework.

Second, notice that the CLR, among other components, is at the center of the circles. The CLR is a crucial part of the foundation because it's the engine that loads and manages the execution of source code.

What Is Visual Basic 2008?

Visual Basic 2008 is one of the programming languages that target the .NET Framework. Like any spoken or written language, Visual Basic has syntax rules and a series of valid words you can use to create your applications. Visual Basic is a popular choice for beginners because some people find the syntax simpler than the syntax of many other programming languages. If you have used an older version of Visual Basic (such as Visual Basic 4.0, 5.0, or 6.0), you'll find some familiar constructs and a familiar user interface (UI) in Visual Basic 2008.

Is Visual Basic 2008 an Object-Oriented Programming Language?

Visual Basic 2008 is a fully fledged object-oriented programming language. Let's talk about what this means.

Object-oriented programming (OOP) is a programming style (or programming paradigm). There are other programming paradigms, such as functional or procedural programming. Languages such as C, Fortran, Pascal, and previous versions of Visual Basic all use functional or procedural programming paradigms. These paradigms focus more on the actions, while OOP focuses more on the data itself.

MORE INFO
With C++ you can develop procedural applications, pure object-oriented applications, or a mix of both.

Applications that use the OOP paradigm are developed using OOP languages (OOPLs). The first OOPLs were introduced in the late 1960s, but they really became popular in the late 1970s. They are widely used today because most people agree that they're easy to learn, use, debug, and maintain. For instance, OOPLs easily represent real-world objects. Visual Basic 2008 is an OOPL as are C#, C++, Java, Smalltalk, Lisp, and others.

Programmers use OOP to write programs that represent the decomposition of real-world problems into modules. Those modules represent real-world objects and are known as *classes* or *types*. You can think of an OOP program as a collection of objects interacting with each other. Using OOP, a programmer defines new types to represent real-world objects, such as a plane, a person, a customer, a dog, or a car. Those types or classes have what are known as *constructors*, which developers use to create objects or instances. An *object* in a program is a unit that represents one instance of a real-world object. It's a self-contained unit because it includes all the data and functionality associated with that object. This means each object created in an application contains all the information that characterizes it (data members or fields) and all the actions (methods) that can access or modify that information.

Here is a simple example in Visual Basic 2008 that defines a *Person* class:

```
1   Public Class Person
2        'Data members
3        Private Name As String
4        Private Address As String
5        Private City As String
6        Private State As String
7        Private ZIP As String
8        Private Country As String
9
10       'Methods
11       Overridable Sub Display()
12           Console.WriteLine(Name)
13           Console.WriteLine(Address)
14           Console.WriteLine(City)
```

```
15          Console.WriteLine(State)
16          Console.WriteLine(ZIP)
17          Console.WriteLine(Country)
18      End Sub
19  End Class
```

MORE INFO

In the example of the *Person* class, you would need to implement properties to access or modify the *Private* fields from outside the class. These types of fields hide data in your class.

This class includes private data members and a *Display* method to print the object's content to the console. The *Sub* method is by default public. The *Overridable* keyword means that a new class derived from this class will be able to write its own implementation of the *Display* method.

Let's use a different example to go over these concepts some more. My dog, Chopin, is an instance of the class *Dog*, and the class *Dog* is a subclass of the *Animal* class. Because Chopin is a dog, he has some behaviors and data that are proper for a dog. But because a dog is also an animal, Chopin also inherits some data and behaviors from the *Animal* class.

This means that the instance *Chopin* of the class *Dog* has data members that characterize him and methods that I can call on that little furry ball. For example, here is the instance information for the *Chopin* object:

Data

- **Breed**   He's a Maltese.

- **Gender**   He's male.

- **Weight**   His weight is 5.5 pounds (2.5 kilograms).

- **Color**   He's white.

- **Name**   His name is Chopin Chabispel.

- **Age**   He's three years old.

Actions

- He speaks (barks).

- He eats.

- He moves.

- He sleeps.

All these data items (breed, gender, weight, color, name, and age) and actions (speak, eat, move, and sleep) characterize him, but they can also characterize any other dog, such as my neighbor's dog, Molly. And if you think about it, those items can characterize any animal. This means that the class *Dog* inherits data members and methods from the class *Animal*.

Let's say you want to develop an application for a veterinary clinic. To cover the cats who come to your clinic, all you must do is create a *Cat* class that also inherits from the class *Animal*. Then each class (*Cat* and *Dog*) could override functionality in the *Animal* class as needed. For instance, for the *Cat* class the *Speak* method would be *meows* instead of *barks*. This means that those *Speak* methods for *Cat* and *Dog* are specializations of the regular animal *Speak* method.

Let's look at the *Person* class example again. This time, I'll also show an *Employee* class that derives from the *Person* class. The *Employee* class derives from the *Person* class by using the keyword *Inherits* followed by the *Person* element. The keyword *Overrides* changes the implementation of the *Display* method.

```
20  Public Class Employee
21      Inherits Person
22
23      Public Level As Integer
24      Public Salary As Integer
25
26      Overrides Sub Display()
27          Console.WriteLine(Name + " is at level " + Level.ToString() +
            " and has a salary of : " + Salary.ToString() + "$")
28          Console.WriteLine("His address is:")
29          Console.WriteLine(Address)
30          Console.WriteLine(City + "," + State + " " + ZIP)
31          Console.WriteLine(Country)
32      End Sub
33  End Class
```

TIP
In this book, you'll notice that some code listings include line numbers. If a line does not include a number, it indicates that the code is a continuation from the previous line. Some code lines can get rather long and must be wrapped to be displayed on the printed page. If you need to type the code in Visual Basic, be sure to put continued lines on a single line.

In this case, the *Employee* class inherits from the *Person* class and therefore gets all the data fields from that base class. The *Employee* class doesn't have to redefine any of the fields in its definition because it gets them automatically from *Person*. So, for the *Employee* class, you must specify only what is different from an instance of the *Person* class. For example, an instance of the *Employee* class would have *Level* and *Salary*, whereas none of the instances of the *Person* class would. The *Display* method for *Employee* could thus add level and salary information to the displayed message when it is called.

This was just a brief introduction to OOP and some of its concepts. Visual Basic 2008 supports all of these concepts and many more. Throughout this book you'll see more OOP concepts, and when you do, I'll highlight them in a "reader aid" information box, as shown in the left margin.

Here's the complete listing used in this section with the addition of the *Customer* class:

NOTE

In .NET, all classes ultimately derive from the *Object* class, even when it is not specified.

```
34  Imports System
35
36  Public Class Person
37      'Data members
38      Public Name As String
39      Public Address As String
40      Public City As String
41      Public State As String
42      Public ZIP As String
43      Public Country As String
44
45      ' Methods
46      Overridable Sub Display()
47          Console.WriteLine(Name)
48          Console.WriteLine(Address)
49          Console.WriteLine(City)
50          Console.WriteLine(State)
51          Console.WriteLine(ZIP)
52          Console.WriteLine(Country)
53      End Sub
54  End Class
55
56  Public Class Customer
57      Inherits Person
58
59      Public ID As Integer
60      Public IsPartner As Boolean
61
62      Overrides Sub Display()
63          Dim partnerMessage As String
64
65          If IsPartner Then
66              partnerMessage = " is a partner"
```

```vbnet
67          Else
68              partnerMessage = " is not a partner"
69          End If
70
71          Console.WriteLine("Customer ID: " + ID.ToString())
72          Console.WriteLine(Name + partnerMessage)
73          Console.WriteLine(Address)
74          Console.WriteLine(City + "," + State + " " + ZIP)
75          Console.WriteLine(Country)
76      End Sub
77  End Class
78
79  Public Class Employee
80      Inherits Person
81
82      Public Level As Integer
83      Public Salary As Integer
84
85      Overrides Sub Display()
86          Console.WriteLine(Name + " is at level " + Level.ToString() + " and
                  has a salary of : " + Salary.ToString() + "$")
87          Console.WriteLine("His address is:")
88          Console.WriteLine(Address)
89          Console.WriteLine(City + "," + State + " " + ZIP)
90          Console.WriteLine(Country)
91      End Sub
92  End Class
```

This is a simple case, but it illustrates some of the basic concepts of OOP.

What Is Visual Basic 2008 Express Edition?

Visual Basic 2008 Express Edition is the tool we will use throughout this book to develop applications that run on Windows. The Express editions of Visual Studio 2008 were designed to focus on productivity. As with the high-end versions of Visual Studio 2008, the Express editions are also what we call *rapid application development (RAD)* tools because their philosophy is geared toward productivity. The Express editions of Visual Studio are easy to use, easy to learn, and streamlined because although they contain mostly the same components, they lack the full breadth of features found in the higher-end versions of Visual Studio. Most features and components in the Express editions were simplified to make the learning curve less steep and to fit the needs of the nonprofessional developer.

The Visual Studio 2008 Express editions were designed with beginner programmers in mind—people like you who are curious about programming and who are looking for an easy way to build Windows applications while learning how to program. Visual Basic 2008 Express Edition is the ideal tool to use to rapidly develop applications for topics you really love or for hobbies you enjoy. You can also use it to help ease your day-to-day job or school tasks. Most important, you can have fun with the tool while you're learning to program.

What Kinds of Applications Can You Build with Visual Basic 2008 Express Edition?

With this version of Visual Studio 2008, you'll be able to create the following types of applications:

- **Windows applications**   These are applications that have a graphical interface with buttons, windows, menus, toolbars, and so on, as in Microsoft Word or Windows Internet Explorer. With this book you'll be able to take full advantage of WPF, which lets you build applications that create a rich user experience while exploiting all the power of your computer. You can also build applications that look like Windows Vista–based applications.

- **Console applications**   These are applications that have no graphical interface and that simply use text to communicate with the user. (Typically, these applications run in a command window or DOS window.)

- **Reusable components or class libraries**   These are groups of tools created to help build other applications.

What you won't be able to build are Web sites and Web services. To create any type of Web application, you will need to get Microsoft Visual Web Developer 2008 Express Edition.

NOTE
We will look into the details of what types of applications fall into these categories in Chapter 3, "Creating Your First Applications."

What Are the Key Features You Need to Know About?

The following list, although not complete, provides the essential features of Visual Basic 2008 Express Edition. At this point, don't worry if you don't understand every feature listed. I'm presenting the features in the list because you'll come across all of them in some way in the fun sample applications you will be creating as you read this book.

Most of the features listed here emphasize the RAD philosophy. Although the idea is to give you an overview of the interesting features that can make your life easier, the names of the features alone are not sufficient to understand what they mean. I've included a brief description giving you the essentials and explaining how they will help you develop applications.

- **Built-in Starter Kits**   The Starter Kits are fully developed applications with best practices and examples to follow. These applications will give you another example on which to base your learning. They will be a good complement to what we are doing in this book. You can find them at *http://msdn2.microsoft.com/en-us/vbasic/ms789080.aspx*.

- **Beginner's targeted documentation and tutorials**   These are a fast and easy way to get information. They also provide samples.

- **IntelliSense**   This feature provides real-time syntax suggestions and even finishes your typing for you. In Visual Studio 2008, IntelliSense, as you will see, is everywhere (it's now called IntelliSense Everywhere), and it provides a more complete and contextual set of suggestions.

- **Code snippets**   Snippets provide code for more than 200 programming tasks to help you complete many common tasks automatically. In addition, code snippets show the recommended way of performing a task. They are directly integrated into the development environment, and they are extensible; that is, anybody can extend the existing snippets or provide new ones. Over time Microsoft will continue to supply new code snippets, and members of online communities will contribute their snippets as well. Code snippet extensibility seems to be a really nice feature that will help people share useful features in online communities.

- ***My* construct**   This new Visual Basic feature provides simple access to popular .NET Framework classes and common tasks. With it you can perform tasks without knowing all the framework internals. These tasks are nicely wrapped and provide you with an easy and clean way of getting things done. Although similar to code snippets, the *My* construct elements have their source code hidden and wrapped in one line of code.

- **Data-enabled applications**   With these applications you can connect to Microsoft SQL Server 2005 Express Edition and add databases and code to access the data in your applications. In addition, a new editor has been added to help you develop applications that use data. As mentioned earlier, LINQ is one of the big new features of .NET 3.5 included with Visual Studio 2008, and you'll see how to use it in Chapter 8, "Managing the Data."

- **Windows Forms Designer and WPF Designer**   With these new tools, you can easily design your Windows application using either Windows Forms or WPF, including features such as snap lines, which make sure your controls are aligned in your form, and autocorrect, which gives you real-time compiler feedback. You won't have to compile your code to know whether you have errors; Visual Basic 2008 will show them to you as you type and even give you potential fixes.

MORE INFO

XAML is also used in Silverlight for Web applications, but this is beyond the scope of this book.

- **XAML Editor**   The XAML Editor lets you edit Extensible Application Markup Language (XAML), which was introduced with .NET 3.0. This new markup language is used extensively in WPF and Windows Workflow (WF) to describe user interface elements in WPF and process logic in WF. (WF is beyond the scope of this book.)

- **XML Web services**   Visual Basic 2008 provides easy-to-use tools and wizards that will help you connect to published XML-based Web services and will help you utilize their functionality.

- **New Windows Forms controls**   These comprise an impressive list of controls—a greater selection than in any previous version of Visual Basic. They will help you create user interfaces that have a professional look and feel.

- **Smart Tags**   Most Windows Forms controls that come with the product include Smart Tags. As in many applications of the 2007 Microsoft Office system, a Smart Tag is represented by a little black triangle, or an icon and a little black triangle, attached to a control. A Smart Tag gives you access to the most common actions you can perform on a control.

- **ClickOnce deployment**   With this feature you can easily publish your applications on the Internet, on a local area network (LAN), on a network share, or on a CD. It also simplifies publishing updates. In this new edition of Visual Studio, you can now use a wizard to handle the Windows Vista User Account Control (UAC) so that your application runs in the lowest user security context it needs. Usually you want to aim your software development on Windows Vista at regular users. This has the effect of reassuring users that your application won't perform unsafe operations without their knowledge.

- **Edit and Continue**   While you are debugging your application, the Edit and Continue feature lets you modify the code, move back and forth in the debugger, re-execute code, add functionality, or fix bugs on the fly without stopping program execution.

- **Debugger visualizers**   While you are debugging your application, the visualizers give you an easy way to get readable representations of your application data. They give you a human-readable representation of the stored data, even for more complex types found in ADO.NET or XML.

- **Community Access and Start pages**   With these features, you can access additional information from online communities and from different sources of online help, including diverse RSS feeds. (RSS can stand for Rich Site Summary or Really Simple Syndication and is a family of XML file formats; it is widely used by the weblog community and news Web sites.)

- **Simplified development environment**   Everything in the development environment was created so that you can easily access key functionality, tools, and objects.

As you can see, Visual Basic 2008 Express Edition includes many nice features to help new programmers develop applications in a fast and fun way. These features will provide guidance even when you're not necessarily sure what syntax or components to use and will greatly expedite learning the product.

In Summary...

You now know that .NET is a framework composed of compilers, tools, languages, debuggers, and an execution engine. The CLR is that execution engine, and it is responsible for loading and executing managed applications. In essence, .NET is like a house with the CLR as the foundation and all other services built on top of it. You also learned that the CLR didn't change with Windows Vista and Visual Studio 2008, but a lot of new building blocks have been added so you can take advantage of features provided by Windows Vista and make developing applications easier.

In addition, you learned that Visual Basic 2008 is an object-oriented programming language that has a simpler syntax than most modern programming languages. You also started to learn what object-oriented programming is and the basics of OOP in Visual Basic 2008.

This chapter gave you the opportunity to hear about the most important features of Visual Basic 2008 Express Edition. In the next chapter, you'll learn how to install Visual Basic 2008 Express Edition.

Chapter 2
Installing Visual Basic 2008 Express Edition

In this chapter, you'll install Microsoft Visual Basic 2008 Express Edition and start getting to know what components are included with it. I'll guide you through all the steps of this installation so that you will be ready to start building applications using Visual Basic 2008 Express Edition right away. In addition, I will talk about some common installation scenarios, give you some tips for installing the product, and cover what to do if the unexpected happens.

The installation process is easy and straightforward, following in the spirit of the Microsoft Visual Studio Express editions.

You have a couple of options for installing Visual Basic 2008, particularly if you've had previous versions installed or if you installed an early (prerelease) version of the product. Before you start the installation, make sure your computer meets the software and hardware recommendations. Review the introduction of this book for all the necessary information. You will also want to be sure that your computer has the latest updates from Windows Updates (*http://windowsupdate.microsoft.com*) and Microsoft Updates (*http://update. microsoft.com*). Installing the latest updates will ensure that your computer has all the latest security updates along with some installation prerequisites before starting the product installation.

If you have an antivirus or antispyware application installed and running, it might prompt you to choose to allow certain setup tasks to proceed. For instance, with the latest Microsoft Windows Defender (*http://www.microsoft.com/athome/security/spyware/software/default. mspx*), I was asked two times to allow certain tasks to proceed, and a few other times the antispyware product recognized the source and simply mentioned it and continued. If you are using a different antispyware application, your experience might vary slightly, but it will bear some similarities to this process. These antivirus and antispyware products are giving you an opportunity to confirm the origin of the product you're about to install. When you're sure it's from Microsoft, let the setup application continue its job by choosing to allow the action.

During the installation, if something goes wrong, you're probably not the only person to encounter the problem. Your first step is to look at the latest Readme information maintained by the setup team on MSDN and follow the steps provided to solve the installation problem. Here is the link: *http://www.microsoft.com/express/support/*.

Side-by-Side Installation

CAUTION

Please make sure you carefully read the article at *http://msdn2. microsoft.com/en-us/vs2008/ bb964521.aspx* before starting the uninstall process!

If you have a previous version of Visual Studio on your computer, say Visual Studio 2002 or Visual Studio 2003, installing Visual Basic 2008 Express Edition (or any Visual Studio 2008 product) will be straightforward. This is considered a *side-by-side* execution, and you can go straight to the "Installing Visual Basic 2008 Express Edition" section about installing the software.

16

Microsoft Visual Basic 2008 Express Edition: Build a Program Now!

Prerelease Versions of Visual Basic 2008 Express Edition

When you uninstall a prerelease version of any software, you might encounter problems. At some point, you might have no choice but to reformat your hard disk and reinstall your operating system. This situation is not uncommon when you work with prerelease software, but there is a solution. Before beginning the uninstall procedure, and as a precautionary measure, be sure to back up all your data. If possible, a good practice is to avoid installing any prerelease versions of any products on your main computer. Using a test machine (or virtual software) will help you avoid losing any important data and won't slow your productivity in the event something goes wrong. You can learn more about the virtual solution that Microsoft offers, called Microsoft Virtual PC 2007, at *http://www.microsoft.com/windows/virtualpc/default.mspx*.

Luckily with Visual Studio 2008, all Community Technology Preview (CTP) and pre–Beta 2 versions were "time-bombed" virtual images provided by Microsoft; therefore, the chance of ruining your main computer has been almost eliminated. You simply have to delete the Virtual PC image provided by Microsoft, and you should be good to go with the released version of the product. But if you have installed Visual Basic 2008 Express Edition Beta 2 and you didn't use a Virtual PC image, you will have to uninstall the beta version before you proceed with installing the released version.

MORE INFO

Because of a new feature called *multitargeting*, you can compile any project to .NET 2.0, .NET 3.0, or .NET 3.5. After successfully installing Visual Basic 2008 Express Edition, you can safely uninstall Visual Basic 2005 Express Edition because with Visual Basic 2008 Express Edition, you can target .NET 2.0 and also get the benefits and new features of Visual Basic 2008 Express Edition.

NOTE

Even though Microsoft doesn't officially support prerelease versions of the software, you will find resources on Microsoft's Web site to help you with installation. In particular, you will find information on how to uninstall (and in what order to uninstall) the products. Look at the forums at the following address for help on uninstalling any Beta 2 installations (you'll need to sign in using a Windows Live ID to get to this article): *http://forums.microsoft.com/msdn/showforum.aspx?forumid=1346&siteid=1.*

Installing Visual Basic 2008 Express Edition

Now that we've addressed a lot of potential issues and your computer is ready, you can proceed with the installation. You will find a companion DVD with this book that contains a full working edition of the product. Simply insert it into any available CD/DVD drive in your system, and follow the steps listed next.

IMPORTANT

If you install Visual Basic 2008 Express Edition on the Windows Vista operating system, you should be prompted by the Windows Vista User Access Control dialog box to give the setup process permission to continue. If you have been using Windows Vista for a while, you have probably seen this dialog box many times. Click Continue to proceed with the installation.

NOTE

You'll have nothing to do but wait at this point. The wait should not be long—less than a minute in most cases, depending on your computer's speed.

MORE INFO

You'll see a check box at the bottom of the License Terms page that enables Visual Studio to receive and display plenty of useful information, such as tips, blogs, and samples about .NET and Visual Basic. If you clear it, you can always select it again after the product is installed by using the Tools menu.

TO INSTALL VISUAL BASIC 2008 EXPRESS EDITION

If autorun is enabled, the installation process should start automatically. If it doesn't start automatically after a few seconds, follow these steps:

1. Click the Start button, and then click Computer.

2. Right-click the CD/DVD drive that has the product media, and select Explore.

3. In the list of files, locate and double-click Setup.hta to start the Installation Wizard.

4. On the Welcome to Visual Studio 2008 Express Editions Setup page, click Microsoft Visual Basic 2008 Express Edition.

Within a few seconds, you should see that the setup program is copying all the necessary installation files to a temporary folder, as shown in Figure 2-1.

When the setup program is done copying the files, the setup application loads into memory. While the application is loading, you'll see an initialization progress bar, as shown in Figure 2-2.

Figure 2-1
Copying setup files locally to a temporary folder

Next, you'll be greeted by the Welcome to Setup page (Figure 2-3), which provides some information about the product and the possibilities you'll have working with it. You can select the check box if you want to send anonymous data about your experience installing the product to Microsoft. This program is totally anonymous, and you can read the policy to see exactly what type of information will be sent. Click Next to continue or Cancel to exit the installation program.

Figure 2-2
Initializing the setup process

To continue the installation process, you must read and accept the license terms (Figure 2-4). Please read the terms carefully to see what you can and can't do with this product. When you have finished and you're ready to accept the license agreement, select the option button that says you have read and accepted the license, and then click Next to continue.

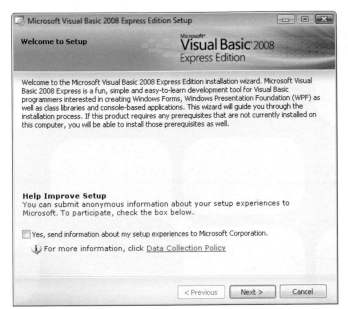

Figure 2-3
Welcome to Setup page

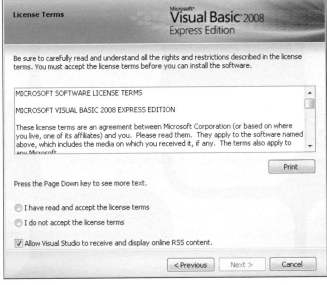

Figure 2-4
License terms

The Installation Options page appears, as shown in Figure 2-5. On this page, be sure to specify that you want access to the Help system (MSDN Express Library) and Microsoft SQL Server 2005 Express Edition.

SQL Server 2005 Express Edition is a relational database management system (RDBMS) with which you can easily manipulate data in your application. This is an important step. For example, if you're creating the DVD collection management application that is included as one of the Starter Kits, all the data related to your DVD collection will need to be stored in a database using SQL Server 2005 Express Edition.

NOTE

The only reason not to install the local MSDN Help or SQL Server 2005 Express Edition is limited hard disk space. Be sure you understand the consequences of your selections. If you don't install MSDN Express Library, you'll need access to the Internet to get help from MSDN Online. If you don't install SQL Server 2005 Express Edition, you won't be able to create applications that need to access other sources of data, such as Microsoft Access database information, XML files, or other types of RDBMS information. In addition, some sample files from this book won't work automatically, and you'll have to perform some manipulations or re-installations to get them to work.

MORE INFO

Silverlight, previously named WPF Everywhere (WPF/E), is a cross-browser, cross-platform plug-in for delivering the next generation of .NET-based media experiences and rich interactive applications for the Web. From a user point of view, Silverlight behaves like Adobe Flash, but Silverlight is richer in terms of what you can do and, more specifically, how you can do it. With Silverlight 2.0, for example, you will be able to use your Visual Basic skills and expertise to develop Silverlight applications. You can find nice samples, documentation, and much more about Silverlight at *http://www.silverlight.net*.

CAUTION

If you choose to install the software in a folder other than the recommended default, you might have problems working with some of the paths and files mentioned later in the book. If you do install in a different location, rest assured I'll give you some cautionary notes whenever you might run into problems.

NOTE

The installation time will vary on the basis of your choices on the previous page. On average, if you selected both MSDN Library and SQL Server 2005 Express Edition, the installation should take about 10 to 30 minutes, depending on your computer's speed.

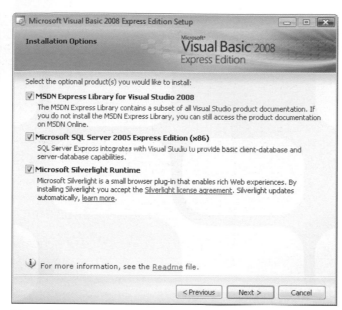

Figure 2-5
Setting your installation options

The last product to install is Silverlight. Although we won't use Silverlight directly in this book, I strongly recommend you install it because you will have a smoother and richer experience on many Web sites. Silverlight 1.0 will not take up a lot of disk space, because it is only a few megabytes.

When you're done with your selections, click Next to continue.

The Destination Folder page appears, as shown in Figure 2-6. This page will ask you where to install the software on your computer. I recommend you use the default location.

Click Install to start the installation. The installation progress bar appears, which means the installation is underway! (See Figure 2-7.) This might be a good time to get something to drink because the installation could take some time.

Figure 2-6
Destination Folder page

Figure 2-7
Installation Progress page

Here is the list of components that will be installed:

 The .NET Framework 3.5   This was the outer circle of the image illustrated in Figure 1-1.

 Visual Basic 2008 Express Edition   This is the tool itself.

 Microsoft SQL Server Compact 3.5   This is a version of SQL Server that lets you, as the developer, embed a compact database on smaller devices, such as Windows Mobile–based phones or even on your Windows–based desktop or laptop.

 MSDN Express Library for Visual Studio 2008   This was described earlier.

 SQL Server 2005 Express Edition   This was described earlier.

When the Setup Complete page appears (see Figure 2-8), you are now finished with the installation. That wasn't too painful, was it? Before you click the Exit button, please read the following notes.

Whenever you install a new application, it's always a good habit to go to Microsoft Update (*http://update.microsoft.com*) or Windows Update (*http://windowsupdate.microsoft.com*) to get all the high-priority updates. Or you can click the Microsoft Update hyperlink from the setup application, as shown in Figure 2-8. I prefer Microsoft Update because you get all the updates you need for all the Microsoft software already installed on your hard disk. You'll get updates for Windows, the Microsoft Office system, SQL Server, Windows Defender, and the .NET Framework along with your hardware drivers updates, all in one stop!

TIP

In the future, more products will be added to the list of products supported by Microsoft Update.

It's also important to verify that your antivirus application and its signatures are up-to-date and that you have updated antispyware installed. Finally, in Control Panel, open the Security Center, and make sure all lights for the firewall, virus protection, automatic updates, and all other security settings are green. If not, address those issues to prevent any security hazards.

Click the Exit button when you are done. If you elected to send the feedback of your installation to Microsoft on exit, the setup application will send it to Microsoft's servers, as shown in Figure 2-9.

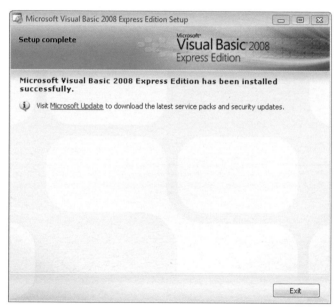

Figure 2-8
Setup Complete page

Figure 2-9
Sending installation feedback to the Microsoft servers

In Summary...

This chapter focused on installing Visual Basic 2008 Express Edition. It addressed most issues you might encounter during the installation, it covered different setup scenarios, and it provided links to MSDN for more help.

After working through this chapter, you should now have the .NET Framework 3.5, Visual Basic 2008 Express Edition, MSDN Express Library for Visual Studio 2008, SQL Server Compact 3.5, Silverlight 1.0, and SQL Server 2005 Express Edition installed and ready to go. Your computer should also be up-to-date with all updates installed and all security settings on green.

Whenever you're ready to explore the integrated development environment (IDE) and write your first two applications, just jump to the next chapter.

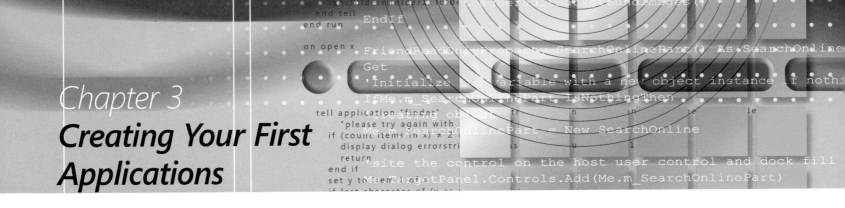

Chapter 3
Creating Your First Applications

You've installed Microsoft Visual Basic 2008 Express Edition, so now it's time to create your first applications. You'll start this chapter by learning about the differences between console applications, Windows applications, and Windows Presentation Foundation (WPF) applications. You'll then look at the integrated development environment (IDE). As its name implies, the IDE is the application that provides all the tools you need to design, plan, develop, and distribute your applications. You could use any text editor, such as Notepad, for example, to create your applications, but in this chapter and for the reminder of the book, you'll be using the IDE.

Most programming books usually start with a fairly simple application called "Hello, World." Your first application will be a simple application as well, but you'll be creating an application that does a little bit more than just say "Hello" to the world. Specifically, you'll learn to create an application that adds two numbers together and outputs a result. With this application you'll also learn about Solution Explorer as well as the documentation and Help system built into Visual Basic 2008 Express Edition.

In this chapter, you'll create two versions of the same application: a console application and a Microsoft Windows application. You might wonder why you even have to worry about the type of application when you're creating a program. Often, the type of application you create depends on the purpose of the application and how users will interact with it.

Sometimes your application doesn't need to have a graphical interface. For instance, some applications need to be executed in a script or a batch file, or they don't need a graphical interface because no user usually interacts with the application except to start it. This type of application is called a *console application* because everything is displayed in a system console window. You might have heard these types of windows referred to by many different names: a *DOS window*, a *command prompt window*, or simply the *command window*. The most common output in a console application is simple text.

Figure 3-1 shows the result of the famous "Hello, World" application as a console application.

> **NOTE**
> Please note that console applications are still executed in Windows but in the console.

> **NOTE**
> Console applications can be written in many different programming languages (C, C++, C#, Visual Basic, and so on) and scripting languages (Perl, Python, JScript, and so on).

```
Administrator: Command Prompt                                    _ □ X
C:\Users\ppelland\Documents\Visual Studio 2008\Projects\Helloworld\Helloworld\bin\Debug>He
lloworld.exe
Hello, World from a Console Application

C:\Users\ppelland\Documents\Visual Studio 2008\Projects\Helloworld\Helloworld\bin\Debug>
```

Figure 3-1
A console application

> **MORE INFO**
> Simple text (also called *ASCII characters*) is the usual output of a console application, but some console applications use ASCII graphic characters. (ASCII stands for American Standard Code for Information Interchange.) An ASCII code is the numerical representation of a character (such as 0 or #) or an action of some sort. Pressing Enter in a word processor to move to a new line of text is an action represented by an ASCII character, for instance. The ASCII graphic character set, also called *extended ASCII characters*, includes vertical lines, vertical double lines, corners, and much more. ASCII characters are sometimes used to create boxes around text in console applications. Unicode characters are similar to ASCII but are not encoded in the same way. They are more extensive and can represent different locales.

Console applications can be much more complex than the "Hello, World" example shown here. In fact, they can have as rich a set of features as Windows applications. The only difference is that they don't have a graphical interface. For example, in corporate data centers, many applications execute all day and night, producing a large amount of data. It would be time-consuming and problematic to rely on people to verify the data. So, data centers are usually highly automated to facilitate this job; they use console applications that produce, manipulate, and verify the data in scripts or batch files.

In contrast to a console application, a *Windows application* has a graphical interface, as shown in Figure 3-2. (This type of application is also called a *Windows Forms application* in .NET.)

These applications are usually accessible from the Windows Start menu, and by default they share some common characteristics, such as a Close button, a Maximize button, and a Minimize button, as shown here:

A third type of application—a *WPF application*—also has a graphical interface and looks similar to a Windows application; however, WPF applications use a completely different set of libraries to generate their executable files. For our work in this chapter, it is enough to say that WPF applications can provide a richer experience and use a different approach for their design.

Figure 3-3 shows a WPF application in action. I will explain them much more fully in Chapter 6, "Modifying Your Web Browser."

Figure 3-2
A Windows application includes a graphical interface.

Maximize

Minimize   Close

Figure 3-3
A WPF application

N O T E

A Windows service is a type of Windows application that runs on Windows in the background; it doesn't have a user interface, doesn't produce any visual out-put, starts when Windows starts, and doesn't even require a user to be logged in to start executing. Windows XP Service Pack 2 (SP2) and the Windows Vista operat-ing system come with roughly four dozen Windows services. For example, one built-in Windows service validates your user name and password at start-up.

Getting Started with the IDE

NOTE

The first time you start Microsoft Visual Basic 2008 Express Edition, it will take some time to load because the IDE is being configured for the first time.

To get started writing the code for the console version of your first application, you'll need to start Microsoft Visual Basic 2008 Express Edition. To do this, follow these three easy steps: click Start, click All Programs, and then click Microsoft Visual Basic 2008 Express Edition.

Before we go further, let's pause and admire the IDE in all its glory. Look at Figure 3-4, and feel the excitement.

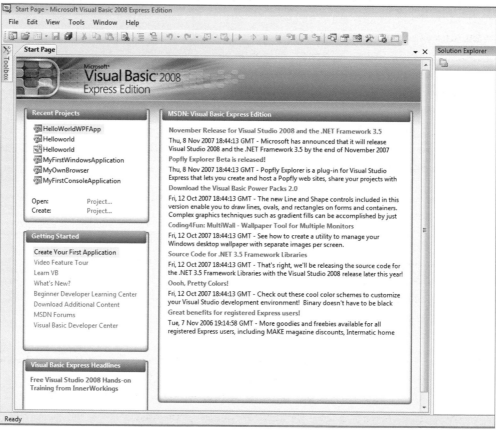

Figure 3-4
The IDE in all its glory

If you're not feeling the excitement yet, you soon will be. The development environment has been designed to make a lot more information available up front and to make you more productive more quickly. From this screen, everything you need to build an application is available in a couple of clicks. This is where you type your code, compile your code, launch the application, find your mistakes and fix them, get help on the syntax, and perform many other tasks. Furthermore, the Visual Basic 2008 Express Edition IDE is designed to generate a lot of code for you so that you have less to type. If you didn't have the IDE and you wanted to write a Windows Forms application, you would have to type a lot more code, and this is prone to errors. With the IDE, most of the actions you'll perform will automatically generate the code for you behind the scenes.

As you spend more time with the IDE, you'll find that there are many ways to perform the same actions. For instance, to complete a specific action, you can use a series of menu choices, you can use a keystroke shortcut, you can click an icon on a toolbar, you can click a hyperlink in a page, or you can right-click and choose an option from a context-sensitive menu. Before diving into our first application and before writing some code, we'll go through each big component of the IDE.

The first page you see when you start the IDE is a really useful one: the Start Page. It contains a lot of useful information:

TIP
The first and only rule of this book is to not be afraid to experiment. Click, look, read, and try whenever possible. This is really the best way to learn. I'll show you some important material, tips, and tricks throughout this book, but my advice to you is to go beyond these examples and just try and try and try.

NOTE
I will show you how and where to look for this generated code in Chapter 5, "Using Rapid Application Development Tools with Visual Basic 2008."

- **Recent Projects pane**   Here you'll get the list of projects or solutions that were recently opened. You can also create a new project or open an existing project that is not in the list.

- **Getting Started pane**   I call this useful pane "Help Central" because if you need quick help, this is one of the best places to get answers. Whether you need help with some Visual Basic constructs, you want to see a list of how-to articles, or you simply want hyperlinks to communities of programmers, you can often find these items in the Getting Started pane of the IDE.

- **Visual Basic Express Headlines pane**   This is where you find specific news about Visual Basic Express Edition from Microsoft. These product headlines deliver special messages specific to Visual Basic 2008 Express Edition and announce new updates, new releases, new code snippets, or anything that needs attention on your part.

NOTE
Some hyperlinks on the Start Page require a live connection to the Internet. So if you are unable to read the hyperlinks, please verify your Internet connection status.

NOTE

The Microsoft Developer Network (MSDN) is a set of online and offline services designed to help developers write applications using Microsoft products and technologies.

NOTE

If you don't see Startup and other settings in the Options dialog box, ensure that you select the Show All Settings check box in the lower-left corner of the Options dialog box.

TIP

If you accidentally close the Start Page and you want to display it, you can always get it back by clicking View, Start Page.

- **MSDN feeds**   This pane of the Start Page includes hyperlinks to articles from one of MSDN's Really Simple Syndication (RSS) feeds. You can configure these articles for any valid RSS feed from the Web. The default is set to the MSDN Visual Basic 2008 Express RSS feed. These articles are usually different from the ones under Visual Basic Express Headlines; occasionally they might be the same, but the articles from MSDN cover not only Visual Basic Express Edition but also topics including Visual Studio Team Systems, Microsoft SQL Server, Web services, and so forth. You can modify the feed by clicking Tools and then Options, expanding Environment, selecting Startup, and updating the Start Page News Channel field with a valid RSS feed of your choice.

Some important components of the IDE are not part of the Start Page:

- **Menu bar**   This is where you can select and perform almost all possible actions related to your projects, files, and Help. The options available change based on the current context. For example, when you don't have a project open, you have fewer menu choices: File, Edit, View, Tools, Window, Community, and Help. When a project is open, the menu choices will also include Project, Build, Debug, and Data.

- **Main toolbar**   This toolbar contains icons that are essentially shortcuts to popular actions that you can also perform by going through the menus.

- **Toolbox**   The Toolbox contains controls that are used in your applications. If you scroll over the Toolbox on the left side of the Start Page, the Toolbox will expand. If you don't have a project open, the Toolbox will be empty. At this point you can think of controls as visual elements in Windows applications that possess a graphical interface. For instance, once a project is opened, the Toolbox will include buttons, labels, text boxes, menus, toolbars, and so on. I'll explain these controls in greater detail in Chapter 5.

- **Solution Explorer**   This feature lists the files and components in your project. If no project is open, it will be empty. You'll learn more about Solution Explorer later in this chapter.

- **Status bar**   The status bar displays a wide variety of information corresponding to the state of certain active operations. For instance, when you load a project, you'll see a

30

Microsoft Visual Basic 2008 Express Edition: Build a Program Now!

message on your screen such as "Loading project c:\blabla\blabla.vbproj from your hard drive." When you're building an application, you'll see something like "Build started," and when the application has finished, you'll see "Build succeeded" or "Build failed" depending on the success of the process.

Building the Projects

From this point on, you'll focus on what you really came here to do: build some projects. Let's start with your first application—the console version of the application that adds two numbers together.

Building a Console Application

We've been talking about what a console application can do and what it will look like, so why don't we build one? In this section, you'll create a simple mathematic application.

TO BUILD A CONSOLE APPLICATION

1. If Visual Basic 2008 Express Edition is not running, start it by clicking Start, All Programs, Microsoft Visual Basic 2008 Express Edition.

   You can choose to start building your application either by clicking the New Project icon on the toolbar, by selecting Create: Project from the Start Page, or by clicking File, New Project on the menu bar.

2. In the New Project dialog box, select Console Application in the Templates section, and type **MyFirstConsoleApplication** in the Name box. The New Project dialog box should be similar to the one in Figure 3-5. Click OK to create the project.

> **TIP**
> For demos and samples, I recommend you type all the source code in the following examples so that you can better understand the concepts involved. However, for longer source code listings, you can also download the completed code samples (*http://www.microsoft.com/mspress/companion/9780735625419*).

> **NOTE**
> By default in Visual Basic 2008 Express Edition when you click OK, projects are created in a temporary location. When you save or close the project, files are saved in Documents\Visual Studio 2008\Projects. (On Windows XP and Windows Server 2003, you'll find them in My Documents\Visual Studio 2008\Projects.) You can change the default project location by clicking Tools, Options, Projects and Solutions and finding the first text box named Visual Studio Projects Location. We'll look into what files are created and what their content is in Chapter 5.

Figure 3-5
Creating a console application using the New Project dialog box

You should now see the IDE in an idle state waiting for you to write the application's code. Your screen should look like the one shown in Figure 3-6.

Getting to Know Solution Explorer

TIP

If you accidentally close Solution Explorer, you can get it back by clicking View, Solution Explorer.

Before you write the code, you need to learn about Solution Explorer. Shown on the right side of the screen in Figure 3-6, Solution Explorer provides an organized view of your projects and all the files associated with them, as well as some useful commands in the form of a toolbar. You'll find all the source code files, the project settings, the resource files (such as the application icon), the configuration files, and so on, in Solution Explorer.

Figure 3-6
MyFirstConsoleApplication without the code

If you want more information about Solution Explorer, you can always do a search in the Help system and product documentation. Before trying to perform a search, please read the next section; you'll learn a lot about all the information that is at your disposal.

TIP
Note that the Start Page is still available; it's simply a separate tab. You can go to any window by clicking a specific tab or by pressing Ctrl+Tab.

Getting Help: Microsoft Visual Studio 2008
Express Edition Documentation

If you want to read more about Solution Explorer, you need to be introduced to Help and the documentation system. You access the documentation by pressing F1 from within Visual Basic 2008 Express Edition or by using the Help menu. The first time you press F1 or use the Help menu, you'll be greeted with the Online Help Settings dialog box, as shown in Figure 3-7.

Figure 3-7
Online Help Settings dialog box

This dialog box prompts you to choose a primary Help source; you can choose online Help as a primary source, local Help as a primary source, or no online Help at all. Think about your options carefully. If you don't have a broadband (cable, DSL, or satellite) Internet connection, I suggest you choose local Help as the primary source; otherwise, choose online Help as your primary source since it is the best source for the latest information.

Once you've made your selection, you'll see the documentation's graphical interface, as shown in Figure 3-8.

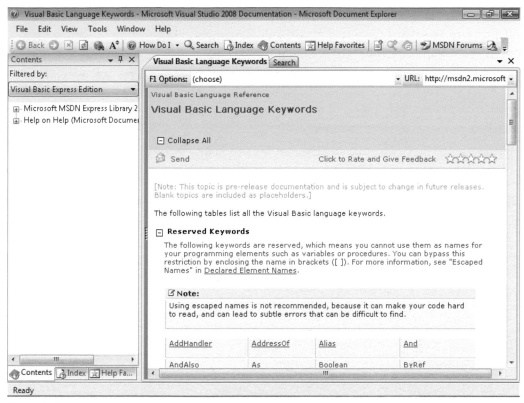

Figure 3-8
Microsoft Visual Studio 2008 Express Edition documentation

The toolbar at the top of the window includes several interesting elements that will help you find exactly what you need. Figure 3-9 shows the most important buttons on the toolbar.

Figure 3-9
Important buttons on the toolbar

For example, let's say you want to learn more about Solution Explorer. Click the Search button on the toolbar, and the search page opens. Enter your search query (in this example, type **Solution Explorer**), and either press Enter or click the Search button. The Help results come from four sources:

- **Local Help** This source is fed by the MSDN Library (part of the product installation) and is installed on your hard disk (if you selected it during installation).

- **MSDN Online** This source contains the most up-to-date information from MSDN Online.

- **Codezone Community** The Codezone Community is a set of Web sites based on Microsoft developer products. To see a list of all Web sites that are researched, click Tools, Options, and then select Online under Help in the list of items at the left. Figure 3-10 shows the dialog box you will see. Notice the list of Web sites on the right that are part of the Codezone Community. In the future, this list might expand to show more sites to provide even better coverage of the community.

  In the same dialog box, you can customize settings related to the Help system. On the General tab, you can set up how the Help system retrieves and presents information. You can set up the international settings to get local Help in the language of your operating system, if available, and get online Help in a predefined list of languages supported by MSDN. You can also view the keyboard shortcut for menu commands used throughout the product (for example, notice that the shortcut for Copy is Ctrl+C) or assign new shortcuts to commands that might not have one already.

Microsoft Visual Basic 2008 Express Edition: Build a Program Now!

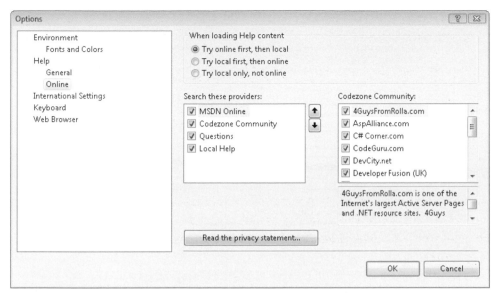

Figure 3-10
Options dialog box with the online settings, including the Codezone Community Web sites

■ **Questions**   This type of query searches the MSDN Online forums (*http://forums. microsoft.com/msdn/*). These forums are hosted by Microsoft and are an excellent source of information because they have questions and answers on topics asked by other programmers of all levels and experience. There's a good chance that somebody has already had the same problem or the same question as you, so your chances of finding an answer to your problem in the MSDN Online forums are good. Furthermore, you can have confidence in the answers you get because answers on the MSDN forums are often validated by Microsoft employees or MVPs. A check mark in a green circle tells you which answer has been validated as correct.

NOTE
MVPs stands for Most Valuable Professionals. MVPs are professionals who are not Microsoft employees but are recognized by Microsoft as experts in their fields.

Coding Your Console Application

Now that you know how to get help if needed, you are ready to code your first console application.

IMPORTANT

Comments in the source code start with a single apostrophe ('). Developers can use comments to explain the operations and purpose of their code so that it is easy to maintain and understand. (It's not rare to see developers staring at their own source code a few months after it was written.) Use comments to explain pieces of code that are more complex or that you think are more important; do not comment pieces of code that are obvious.

TIP

You can also save your project by pressing Ctrl+S to save the current file or by pressing Ctrl+Shift+S to save all the files.

TO CODE A CONSOLE APPLICATION

1. To begin, type the following code in your code window (minus the line numbers):

```
1   Module Module1
2       ' This application will take two numbers and display the sum
3       Sub Main()
4           ' Declaring two integer variables that will hold the 2 parts
5           ' of the sum and one integer variable to hold the sum
6           Dim number1, number2, sum As Integer
7
8           ' Assigning two values to the integer variables
9           number1 = 10
10          number2 = 5
11          ' Adding the two integers and storing the result in the sum variable
12          sum = number1 + number2
13
14          ' Displaying a string with the 2 numbers and the result.
15          Console.WriteLine("The sum of " & number1.ToString() & " and " &
                number2.ToString() & " is " + sum.ToString())
16      End Sub
17  End Module
```

2. Now that the code is in the window, you can save your work by clicking the Save button. This will save the current file. Or you can click the Save All button to save all the modified files in the project.

3. Now it is time to build (or *compile*) the application. Click the Build menu, and then click Build MyFirstConsoleApplication.

   If you typed the code exactly as it appears, you should see the message "Build succeeded" in the status bar at the bottom of the window (see Figure 3-11). If something went wrong, you'll see errors in the Error List (as shown in Figure 3-12). If you typed the code and have errors, try copying and pasting the code from the completed code samples (*http://www.microsoft.com/mspress/companion/9780735625419*) instead of typing it. Then build the code again.

Figure 3-11
Status bar with "Build succeeded" message

	Description	File	Line	Column	Project
⊗ 1	Name 'Consle' is not declared.	Module1.vb	16	9	MyFirstConsoleApplication

Figure 3-12
Error List with errors

Learning to Read Code

I will explain a lot of the source code in this book, but after explaining some topics more than once (or twice), I'll usually explain only the new material. To learn more about the code, you can read the helpful comments I've included in the application source code.

In addition, at the end of each chapter, I will include hyperlinks that point to articles, videos, and white papers, and I will often include keywords to help you search for more information in the online Help. That should help you progress in learning the language and .NET in general. Although this book is showing you what you can do with the product and the steps to get there, it's not a book on object-oriented programming (OOP) or the Visual Basic language itself. You can expand your knowledge even further by reading the code comments and investigating the links and keywords presented.

In Chapter 7, "Fixing the Broken Blocks," you'll learn about all the debugging techniques you can use when you get an error.

4. To see the execution results of your application, click the Start Debugging button in the main toolbar (or hit F5).

Wow! That was fast, wasn't it? You probably saw a command window for a few seconds, and then it disappeared. It didn't leave you a lot of time to see whether your application displayed the expected output. In the next section, you'll look at a new way of running your application to solve this problem. To do this, you'll need to customize the IDE.

Customizing the IDE

You can easily customize the IDE to fit your needs. Here, you want to execute your application and then have the application pause automatically at the end of the last instruction to give you as much time as you need to view the output. You'll do this by adding an icon and its attached command to the main toolbar and to the Debug menu. The name of the command you'll add to the IDE is Start Without Debugging.

TO CUSTOMIZE THE IDE

1. Click the Tools menu, and then click Customize.

2. In the Customize dialog box, select the Commands tab.

3. In the Categories area on the left side of the window, select Debug.

4. Scroll down in the Commands area, and select Start Without Debugging.

   Your screen should now look like the one in Figure 3-13.

   Now you must add the command to the Debug menu. To do that, drag Start Without Debugging from the Commands area, and drop it on the Debug menu. (Figure 3-14 shows a "before" and "after" view of this process.) Now repeat these steps except this time drop the command on the toolbar to the right of the Start Debugging button. (Figure 3-15 shows a "before" and "after" look at the toolbar.) When finished, click Close in the Customize dialog box.

NOTE

Both Figure 3-14 and Figure 3-15 have the "before" version toward the left and the "after" version toward the right, overlapping the "before" version.

Figure 3-13
Customize dialog box with Start Without Debugging selected

Figure 3-14
Before and after customizing the Debug menu with the Start Without Debugging command

Figure 3-15
Before and after customizing the tool-bar with the Start Without Debugging command

To make sure the customization worked, click the new menu item in the Debug menu or the new icon on the toolbar. (Or, press the keyboard shortcut Ctrl+F5.) You should see a command prompt window with the expected output, which is the string "The sum of 10 and 5 is 15." You should also see the message "Press any key to continue," as shown in Figure 3-16.

Figure 3-16
Command prompt window with the expected result and a message indicating a paused execution

As you probably realize by now, the effect of the new command is to display the "Press any key to continue" message and pause the execution after the last instruction executes. Press any key to close the command prompt window and return to the IDE. When you're done, you can close the project by clicking File, Close Project. You'll be prompted to save or discard your changes. Click Save, and then if the name and location are fine, click Save again in the Save Project dialog box.

Creating a Windows Application

You just built a console application. The next step is to develop the same application but as a Windows application. What you will develop is a real Windows application, but it won't do much. You'll create a fully functional Windows application in Chapter 5.

TO BUILD A WINDOWS APPLICATION

1. When creating the console application, you saw the New Project dialog box. Open it again by clicking File, New Project.

2. This time, select Windows Forms Application in the Templates section, and type **MyFirst-WindowsApplication**. Make sure your screen looks like the one in Figure 3-17, and then click OK.

Figure 3-17
Creating a Windows application using the New Project dialog box

You'll immediately see that the result of this operation is quite different for the Windows application process than it was for the console application process. You should see the Windows Forms Designer, as displayed in Figure 3-18.

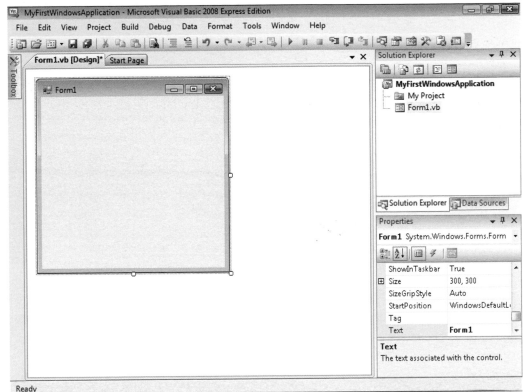

Figure 3-18
IDE with the Windows Forms Designer and an empty form

3. On the left side of the IDE, move your mouse over the Toolbox to open it. Click the plus (+) sign next to Common Controls. You'll see a list of form controls that are common in a Windows application.

4. Drag the Button control to the designer surface. Your form should look like the one in Figure 3-19.

   You now have a full and valid Windows application without having written a single line of code. The application doesn't do anything very useful at this point, but it works! You can easily verify this by running the application. Just hit F5 to see for

Figure 3-19
Windows Forms Designer surface with a Button control

Chapter 3: Creating Your First Applications

yourself. This is part of the magic of using the Visual Studio IDE environment for pro-gramming instead of using a text editor such as Notepad. Visual Studio writes a lot of code for you, and in Chapter 5, we'll look at some of the activity that's taking place behind the scenes to make it appear like magic. When you have finished, click the Close button on the form to return to the IDE.

5. Double-click the button on the designer surface. You'll get the familiar source code win-dow but with different content this time. For now, type or copy the code between *Sub Main()* and *End Sub* from the console application you created previously and add it to the *Button1_Click* method, as shown in Figure 3-20. (You'll learn more about this method and the whole process behind the double-click in Chapter 4, "Creating Your Own Web Browser in Less Than Five Minutes.")

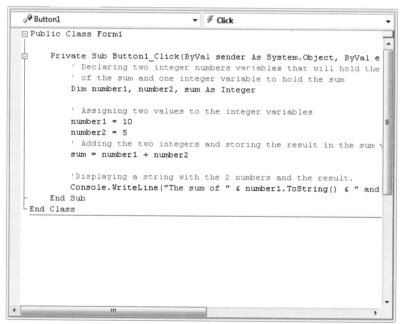

```vb
Public Class Form1

    Private Sub Button1_Click(ByVal sender As System.Object, ByVal e
        ' Declaring two integer numbers variables that will hold the
        ' of the sum and one integer variable to hold the sum
        Dim number1, number2, sum As Integer

        ' Assigning two values to the integer variables
        number1 = 10
        number2 = 5
        ' Adding the two integers and storing the result in the sum
        sum = number1 + number2

        'Displaying a string with the 2 numbers and the result.
        Console.WriteLine("The sum of " & number1.ToString() & " and
    End Sub
End Class
```

Figure 3-20
Button-click method with the code from our previous example

6. In the source code, find the words *Console.WriteLine*, and replace them with the words *MessageBox.Show*. Then build and execute the application by hitting F5.

7. When the form opens, click the button, and you'll see the result of your application: a message box with the same string you saw in the console application. It should look like Figure 3-21. Click OK in the message box, and then quit the program by clicking the Close button on the main form.

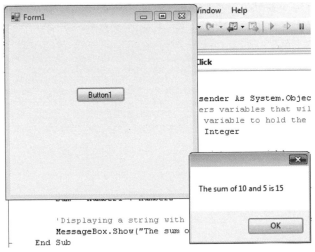

Figure 3-21
Output of MyFirstWindowsApplication

Congratulations! You just created your first two applications: a console application and a Windows application.

Keywords and Links to More Information

If you want to read more about some topics covered in this chapter, simply create a search query by pressing F1 and then type the following keywords: declaring variables *and* string concatenation.

The videos from MSDN are another good source of information. These videos were specifically created to cover Visual Basic 2005 Express Edition, but they are for the most part still applicable to creating your first applications using the 2008 version. You can find the video for Lesson 1, which covers getting started with Visual Basic Express Edition, at the following location: http://msdn2. microsoft.com/en-us/beginner/ bb308737.aspx.

In Summary...

In this chapter, you learned some key information that will help you build on the skills you started developing in the previous chapters. You learned the differences between console applications, Windows applications, and WPF applications. You started Visual Basic 2008 Express Edition, explored the IDE, and learned its major components. In addition, you created two versions of the same application: a console application and a Windows application. While learning about console applications, you also learned what Solution Explorer is as well as how to search and use the product documentation and the Help system.

In the next chapter, you'll build on this knowledge and write a simple Web browser.

Chapter 4

Creating Your Own Web Browser in Less Than Five Minutes

Now that you've gotten a little experience creating simple applications in Microsoft Visual Basic 2008 Express Edition, you'll build a more complicated application in this chapter and finish it in Chapter 6, "Modifying Your Web Browser." In this chapter, you'll start with the basic framework of the application; in the next two chapters, you'll continue to learn new features and then use them to enhance your project.

Specifically, in this chapter you'll learn how to build your own basic Web browser, and you'll be able to do it in five minutes or less!

In the previous chapter, you created a project to hold your source code. I'll now take a moment to explain what a project is and what information it contains. A *project* is a container for all the items in your application, such as forms, source code, and resources. It also stores important configuration data that belongs to the application as a whole, such as the location of the executable (that is, binaries) on your hard disk, the version information, and many more settings that affect the characteristics of your application. For instance, a project stores programmer-defined application settings that are important for the user experience. Users love to customize their software environment to reflect their comfort level and personal styles, for example. You've probably set up specific user preferences in Windows Internet Explorer, such as your home page address, your home page settings, which toolbars are displayed, whether your toolbars are locked in size, and so forth. A typical use of application settings in a project is to make sure the application can preserve user customizations from one execution to another.

In Chapter 6, you'll learn about some of the most important settings stored in the project configuration file and how to use them in your application. In the final chapter of this book, you will use programmatic techniques to preserve the user's settings and customizations.

The name you choose when you create your application becomes the project's name. It also becomes the default folder name on your hard disk where your application is stored when you save it, and this name becomes the default namespace of your application. A *namespace* is used to organize the classes in a program in a single, logical hierarchical structure. It does the same for any other types you might define. The creation of a namespace also helps prevent naming collisions. What is a naming collision? Let's look at an example to illustrate this concept.

Suppose a company called AdventureWorks wrote a new Windows Forms class named *ANewForm*. The company would create a namespace called *AdventureWorks* and put its *ANewForm* class in it to uniquely name the class. The fully qualified name of a class is always composed of the namespace followed by a dot and then the name of the class or classes. Therefore, AdventureWorks's unique class would be *AdventureWorks.ANewForm*.

Now let's suppose you are creating a new project using Visual Studio and decide to name your project MyLibrary. Visual Studio would then create for you a namespace called *MyLibrary*. Suppose you then define a new class and name it *ANewForm*. You might not be aware that a company called AdventureWorks also called its new class using the same name. Even though AdventureWorks might be performing completely different tasks with its class, a problem could arise because the two classes are named the same.

Now suppose you're trying to use both classes called *ANewForm* in your new application. If you simply use *ANewForm*, the compiler will not be able to determine which *ANewForm* class you want to use—the one from your library or the one from the AdventureWorks library; this is a *naming collision*. By prefixing the class name with the namespace name, you tell the compiler exactly which class you want to use (*AdventureWorks.ANewForm* or *MyLibrary.ANewForm*).

What Is the Design Layout?

You will soon create a new design layout in the form designer. In doing so, you'll be creating what the application contains and how its content is presented when the user executes the application.

To accomplish this phase of a project, you typically do not need to type a great deal of code; as explained later in this chapter, Visual Studio takes care of this code for you. You have to worry mostly about how your application looks. When you're done designing all the visual aspects to your liking, your next task usually involves attaching the source code to your visual layout so that your application reacts to and acts upon the user's input.

In this chapter, you will complete the basic layout. You will learn more advanced layout techniques in the following chapters. Let's start the Web browser project now.

To Create a Simple Web Browser

1. Start Visual Basic 2008 Express Edition by clicking Start, All Programs, and then Microsoft Visual Basic 2008 Express Edition.

2. Create a new Windows Forms Application project using any of the techniques shown in the previous chapters; for instance, you can use either the File menu or the New Project icon in the toolbar. Name the new application MyOwnBrowser.

3. On the design surface, you'll see the empty form with a title bar named Form1. Click the title bar once. Look at the Properties window on the bottom right of the IDE, as shown in Figure 4-1.

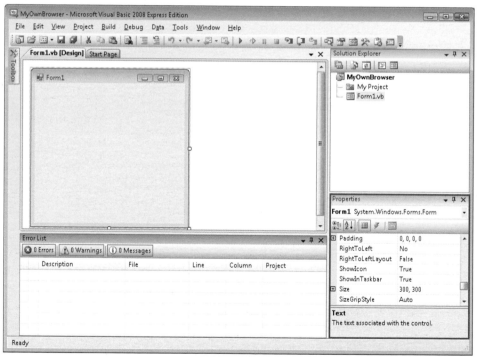

Figure 4-1
Properties window for the MyOwnBrowser application form control

Microsoft Visual Basic 2008 Express Edition: Build a Program Now!

We'll be using most of the properties you see listed here. Right now what is important for you to understand is that most of these properties influence how the control you have selected behaves or what it looks like when you execute your application.

For all the samples in this book, I suggest you sort the Properties window in ascending alphabetical order; it will be much easier to find properties that I reference in the examples. To sort the properties in ascending alphabetical order, click the Alphabetical button in the Properties window toolbar. The other option is to arrange the properties by categories, but this might slow you down as you progress through this book.

Whenever you select a property, you'll see a brief description of its usage at the bottom of the Properties window. Refer to Figure 4-1 as an example. In this case, the *Text* property is selected, and at the bottom of the Properties window, you can see a succinct message describing the function of the *Text* property.

As mentioned in Chapter 3, "Creating Your First Applications," my best advice for learning this software is to try, try, and try again. Visual Basic 2008 Express Edition comes with a variety of tools and therefore many possibilities. You will learn to use most of these tools by performing the exercises in this book, but it's impossible to learn all the variations and possibilities if you don't do some exploring on your own. With that in mind, to understand the effect of changing a particular property, try all the possible values. Each time you modify a property, build and verify the execution. However, don't make more than one change at a time. If you do, it will be difficult for you to know which one of your changes actually triggered a visual modification. By exploring possibilities one at a time, you'll be able to see the effect of your changes immediately.

4. Make sure you have selected the form control named Form1 as directed in step 3, and then modify the properties using the values in Table 4-1. The property name to modify is located in the left column, and the value to which to set the property is located in the right column. You may have already completed this step, but to facilitate your data entry, verify that you have sorted the properties in ascending alphabetical order.

IMPORTANT

Some properties have a plus (+) sign beside them, which means it's a tree view property. Whenever you click the +, you'll expand this property to display the property's attributes, which you will then be able to set. Whenever you are asked to enter values for properties that are in a tree view, I will use the notation structure *Size:Width*, which refers to the *Size* property and the *Width* attribute.

Property	Value
Text	My Own Browser
Size:Width	640
Size:Height	480

Table 4-1
Form Properties to Change

TIP

To add a control to a form, you need to perform a drag-and-drop operation. This means you'll move your mouse pointer to the Toolbox, drag the desired control to the designer surface, and drop the control onto it.

You'll now add three Windows Forms controls to your browser application: a text box control in which to enter the destination URL, a button control to navigate to the Web page, and a WebBrowser control in which the Web page content will be displayed.

5. Drag a WebBrowser control to the designer surface. The WebBrowser control is located in the Toolbox on the left side of the IDE; it's the last control in the Common Controls section.

   By default, this control will fill the designer surface entirely. Because you don't want that behavior for this particular application, click the black triangle, as shown in the left margin, which will produce the content of a Smart Tag. In this particular example, the Smart Tag will help you undock the control from its parent container (the form). Click the Smart Tag, and select Undock in the Parent Container.

6. Expand the control so it occupies almost the entire designer space. To do this, click any of the control handles to change its size.

7. Select the WebBrowser control by clicking anywhere on the control. Then go to the Properties window, and modify the values for all the properties listed in Table 4-2. Modify the values in the same way you modified the form controls in step 4.

Property	Value
(Name)	myBrowser
Size:Width	607
Size:Height	385
Location:X	12
Location:Y	12

Table 4-2
WebBrowser Control Properties to Change

8. Drag a text box control and a button control from the Toolbox's Common Controls section so that your form looks like Figure 4-2. Change the properties of the controls as you did with the WebBrowser control in step 7. Select one control at a time, and modify its properties with the data in Table 4-3.

9. At this point, you have a complete Web browser–congratulations! You can compile and execute your application by pressing F5.

If you followed the previous steps exactly, your application should now be running. Because we didn't code any functionality, entering a URL and hitting the GO button will not do anything.

Figure 4-2
MyOwnBrowser application

Control	Property	Value
Text box	(Name)	txtURL
Text box	Location:X	12
Text box	Location:Y	411
Text box	Size:Width	526
Text box	Size:Height	20
Button	(Name)	btnGo
Button	Location:X	544
Button	Location:X	411
Button	Text	GO

Table 4-3
Controls, Properties, and Values

You first have to "wire up" the controls to the functionality that they will perform. I will use an analogy to explain this fundamental concept. A light bulb by itself is not a useful piece of hardware. To obtain light from it, you need to connect two wires carrying electricity. Similar to what an electrician would do to create this electrical circuit, you need to attach, or *wire*, the control and the action together by writing code to handle the event of clicking the GO button. Keep this analogy in mind when you see references to the term *wire* or *wiring* in this book.

Before we wire up the click action to the button, I'll explain the line of code you'll add in the following instructions, and I'll explain how it relates to the OOP concepts previously introduced in Chapter 1, "Introducing Microsoft Visual Basic 2008 Express Edition."

When you dropped the controls onto the designer surface, you created instances of the class represented by those controls. For example, when you dropped the WebBrowser control, you created an instance of the class *System.Windows.Forms.WebBrowser* that you then named *myBrowser*. The *WebBrowser* class has many methods, and the *Navigate* method is the one you'll use. As its name implies, this method allows the *WebBrowser* class to navigate to a URL. A method in Visual Basic can be a subroutine or a function. The URL is passed as an argument to the *Navigate* method. An argument, also called a *parameter*, is used to pass data to a method.

The argument in this case is the text the user will enter in the instance of the *System.Windows.Forms.TextBox* class that you appropriately named *txtURL*. To retrieve the content of the text box control named *txtURL*, you use the *Text* property of that control. A property enables you to set or retrieve the content of a data member in a class without accessing the data member directly. That way, the provider of the class (for example, Microsoft) can modify the implementation of the *Text* property without concerning the user with the implementation details. In OOP, this is called *encapsulation*. You can compare this process to a person driving a car: you don't need to know how the engine and transmission work to drive the car. Another good example is the *Navigate* method. You don't need to know how it's implemented; you simply want it to do its job. As mentioned earlier, many things are happening when you design a form with Visual Studio. You have seen that you don't need to create any of the classes or instances representing your controls because Visual Studio is doing all of that for you!

TO WIRE THE CLICK ACTION TO A BUTTON

1. Close the running application, and return to the IDE. Double-click the button control. You'll see the code window, as shown in Figure 4-3.

```
btnGo                                    ▼   ⚡ Click                                    ▼
⊟ Public Class Form1

  ⊟      Private Sub btnGo_Click(ByVal sender As System.Object, ByVal e As System.EventArgs) H

         End Sub
  └ End Class
```

Figure 4-3
Code window for the btnGo_Click *event*

If you terminated the execution of your application properly, you should see the source code window with the *btnGo_Click* event template. When you double-clicked the button control, you signaled Visual Studio that you wanted to wire the click action to the button control. Typically, each control can trigger multiple events depending on which behavior you want to intercept with your code. Each control has a default event that becomes available to the programmer for coding by double-clicking the control on the designer surface. In this case, Visual Studio created the *Click* event template so that you could enter the following code.

2. Type the following code at the cursor:

```
myBrowser.Navigate(txtURL.Text)
```

3. Press F5 to compile and execute the application. If you named your controls correctly in step 8 in the previous exercise and entered the line of code as shown in step 2 of this exercise, you should now have your own Web browser application that takes you to a Web page when you enter a URL. Of course, you won't have all the bells and whistles of Internet Explorer, but be patient—we're getting there. Try going to your favorite URLs to see whether your browser is working as expected. For instance, I went to *http://www.microsoft.com*, and it worked just fine! You can see the result in Figure 4-4.

> **NOTE**
> If you try to type some code and it doesn't work, your application is probably still running. If you don't close the application and you return to Visual Basic, you won't be able to modify the source code. A good way to verify that you have closed and terminated the application is to look in the Visual Basic Express Edition title bar. If you see the name of your application followed by the word *(running)*, this means your application is still active and you won't be able to add code. If you try to add code, the status bar will report that you are in read-only mode with the following message: "Cannot currently modify this text in the editor. It is in read-only."

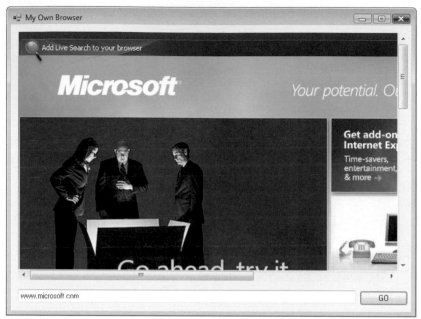

Figure 4-4
MyOwnBrowser showing the Microsoft.com Web site

Putting It All Together

IMPORTANT

Before moving on, I invite you to look at a video from the MSDN Web site that talks about object-oriented programming. You've read a good introduction to OOP both in this chapter and in Chapter 1. To understand the concept from another angle, navigate to *http://msdn2.microsoft.com/ en-us/beginner/bb308752.aspx*, and view Lesson 6, Parts 1 and 2.

You've just seen that when you drag a control to the design surface, you're actually creating an object of that control class. When you're naming the control in the Properties window, you're actually assigning a name to the variable you've just created—which is exactly what you did for the three controls used in your browser. In fact, this is why you want to give your controls meaningful names so that you can use them later programmatically.

As you now know, a great deal of activity was taking place when you dropped controls on the designer surface. To help you understand what took place in the background, we talked about important OOP concepts behind the line of code you added to respond to the click event.

Now that you've run the application, here is a list of questions you may have:

■ What happens if I put nothing in the text box and hit Enter?

■ What happens if I enter an invalid URL?

■ What happens if I enter anything I feel like?

My answer to you is simply, "Try it. Try it now." The real deal is that your Web browser will actually behave like any other Web browser and will navigate to whatever URL is typed in the text box. If you don't type anything, clicking the GO button will have no effect. If you type something that isn't a URL, the browser control will come back with a Page Not Found or Code 404 page.

Now is your time to experiment. Remember this book's rule: try, try, try. Play with it. Change some of the properties, and see the results at run time. Although we haven't used many features yet, you'll add more in Chapter 6. This project is far from over! By adding new features, you'll arrive at a point where your application will start to look much more familiar.

MORE INFO

Philosophies differ when it comes to naming the variable that represents controls on the design surface. In this book, I'll use up to three letters to describe and identify the control type by looking at its name, such as *btn* for a button control. The variable name then becomes *btnGo*. I will introduce the list when I talk about common controls in Chapter 5, "Using Rapid Application Development Tools with Visual Basic 2008."

Links to More Information

Some good sources of information are the videos from MSDN that were specifically created to cover Visual Basic 2005 Express Edition but that are still applicable. The videos for Lessons 2 and 7 cover some of the topics you have just learned and will provide you with another point of view. You can find the videos for Lessons 2 and 7 by typing the following hyperlink: http://msdn2.microsoft.com/en-us/beginner/bb308734.aspx.

In Summary...

In this chapter, you learned how to build a Web browser.

- You added more than one control to the designer surface.
- You set properties in the Properties window.
- You wired an event to a control and learned how to add code that will execute when the event is triggered.

With this example, you saw many OOP concepts in action by using only one line of code. You added the code to respond to the button click event by calling the *Navigate* method of your Web browser object. Your Web browser navigated to a URL passed in as an argument to the *Navigate* method. The argument for the *Navigate* method was passed in using the text box control's *Text* property. Everything was completed and fully working just by tweaking some properties and adding only one line of code! That's what I call productivity.

In the next chapter, you'll continue this process by learning more about the major features of Visual Basic 2008 Express Edition. You'll become more productive at developing applications by learning about features such as IntelliSense, snap lines, code snippets, Smart Tags, the *My* namespace, and much more.

Chapter 5

Using Rapid Application Development Tools with Visual Basic 2008

In Chapter 4, "Creating Your Own Web Browser in Less Than Five Minutes," you started building your own Web browser, and in Chapter 6, "Modifying Your Web Browser," you'll add to its capabilities. But before you do that, I'll introduce some Microsoft Visual Basic 2008 features that will help you develop your Windows programming knowledge and skills. In this chapter, we'll look into some of the more useful rapid application development (RAD) features of Visual Basic 2008 Express Edition.

> **NOTE**
>
> You can find all the RAD features described in this chapter in every edition of Visual Studio 2008. So if you already know how to use these features in Express Edition and decide to explore any of the other editions of Visual Studio 2008, you'll find it much easier to switch and be productive.

Snapping and Aligning Controls Using Snap Lines

TIP

When you have many controls to drop on the designer surface, you can save some time by "pinning" down the Toolbox so that it stays open. To turn off the AutoHide feature so that the Toolbox stays open, click the Auto Hide button (with the pushpin icon) on top of the Toolbox. To turn on the AutoHide feature, click the button again.

Not being a very skilled user interface designer myself, I've always had problems working on a program with many controls to align. Even more difficult was trying to get the alignment right the first time I dropped the controls onto the form. I've always had to go to the Properties window and align the controls manually by entering their x and y coordinates, which slows down the development process quite a bit! One of the philosophies the Visual Basic 2008 team had in mind when creating this awesome product was to make sure you didn't have to perform multiple steps at several different places to accomplish a simple task. And they succeeded with a lot of important features built into the designer; one of these is the snap lines feature with which you can easily align objects on the designer surface. Let's do an exercise so you can see the snap lines feature in action.

TO CREATE A NEW WINDOWS FORM USING SNAP LINES

1. Start Visual Basic 2008 Express Edition by clicking Start, All Programs, Microsoft Visual Basic 2008 Express Edition. Create a new Windows Forms Application project by using any of the techniques shown in the previous chapters (using either the File menu or the New Project icon in the toolbar). Name the new application TestProject.

2. You should see the designer surface. If you don't, right-click the filename Form1.vb in Solution Explorer, and select View Designer. Then, using the Toolbox, drag three text box controls and three label controls to the design surface.

3. Stack the label controls vertically. A thin blue line (a *snap line*) appears on either the right side or the left side of the labels to help guide the alignment. When the labels are aligned correctly, release the label control.

   As shown in Figure 5-1, a small blue horizontal line also appears to the left of the label control. This line represents the minimum space between a control and another control or between a control and its container.

Figure 5-1
Snap lines in action with two label controls

4. After aligning the labels vertically, do the same with the text boxes immediately to the right of each label. The designer surface should look like the one shown in Figure 5-2.

5. Notice that the labels are aligned with the bottoms of the text box controls. For a cleaner appearance, the labels should align with any text that will be entered in the text boxes. To align the labels correctly, move each label until you see a horizontal fuchsia line instead of a blue line, as shown in Figure 5-3. In Figure 5-4, Label1 and Label2 have been properly aligned with the baseline of the corresponding text box contents, but Label3 is still aligned with the bottom of the text box.

Figure 5-2
All the controls are now aligned

Figure 5-3
Example of alignment with the common text baseline

IMPORTANT

Do not close the test project; you'll need it for the sections that follow. If you close the test project and Visual Basic 2008 Express Edition and then re-open them later, you might lose the current view and your form, and code might not show up automatically. If you do happen to close the test form, click the View Code button on the Solution Explorer toolbar to view the code for the selected form, or click the View Designer button to open the designer for the selected form. Alternatively, you can right-click the form filename, in this case Form1.vb, and then select View Code to view the source code or View Designer to open the design surface.

Figure 5-4
Runtime execution of an alignment problem. The bottom label is aligned with the bottom of the text box but not its content.

Using IntelliSense—Your New Best Friend!

NOTE

As a beginner, one of the toughest aspects of programming to learn is the syntax, including knowing when you can use a particular keyword, and so on. Well, IntelliSense in Visual Basic 2008 Express Edition really gives you a hand. It's smart enough to bring you only those suggestions that you can use in the context you are in and therefore removes a lot of potential errors for using a construct in the wrong place.

IntelliSense is one of the greatest tools developed for both beginner and experienced programmers. This feature provides contextual language references within the code editor and can even complete typing for you. This means you can get immediate code syntax help specific to the code you're writing without leaving the code editor. For example, if you're inside a form and you ask IntelliSense for help (you'll see how in a minute), you'll get access to code constructs that make sense for that particular form. You've already experienced IntelliSense while doing the previous examples without really knowing that's what you were using. With Visual Basic 2008, the team has improved IntelliSense even more. In fact, it has improved so much that it has a new name: IntelliSense Everywhere. IntelliSense Everywhere improves productivity compared to Visual Basic 2005 by reducing the number of keystrokes you have to type. Now let's see in detail what IntelliSense Everywhere is.

Using IntelliSense as You Go

In Visual Basic 2008, IntelliSense helps you as you type by adding new kinds of helper functionality. For instance, it now contains the Visual Basic language keywords. For example, keywords such as *Dim* and *As* and all other Visual Basic reserved keywords are now included in IntelliSense.

Figure 5-5 shows an example from the project currently open in the code editor. As soon as I typed **Di**, IntelliSense reduced the number of possibilities to one, *Dim*. IntelliSense was able to detect the context in which I was working when I started typing and present the most logical choice. Another great new feature of IntelliSense shown in this figure is that it provides you with help on the selected keyword or type in the form of a tooltip in the IDE.

Figure 5-5
IntelliSense detects the most logical choice based on the context.

Along the same lines, Figure 5-6 shows how IntelliSense narrows down the number of choices based on the context and the libraries available. The figure shows that when I typed the letters **Open**, IntelliSense narrowed down my logical choices. I had to type only five letters, **OpenF**, to find the *OpenFileDialog* class out of hundreds of possible types in the libraries. This greatly helps reduce the number of keystrokes and keeps errors to a minimum.

Figure 5-6
IntelliSense narrows down the options based on the context.

TIP
As you code bigger projects, it will be common for IntelliSense to hide pieces of code that you need to see. In earlier versions of Visual Basic, the code would be hidden underneath the IntelliSense window, and if you wanted to use the information, you had to remove the window by moving the cursor or the mouse, then reading, and then doing it again. Now you can simply hold down the Ctrl key, and the IntelliSense window will become transparent, allowing you to see underneath.

Another nice feature is that you even get help on your own variables in IntelliSense, as shown in Figure 5-7. As you'll see throughout this book, IntelliSense is smart and helpful but not intrusive.

Figure 5-7
A user-defined variable is available in IntelliSense.

Using IntelliSense Filtering: Removing the "Uncommon"

You might have also noticed that when the IntelliSense window appears, you have two tabs at the bottom: Common and All. These are called *sticky tabs* because they reset the default view when you click them. These tabs are also part of the feature called IntelliSense Filtering. With IntelliSense Filtering, you can adjust the level of detail that IntelliSense supplies in the code editor. When you select the Common tab, IntelliSense filters out most uncommon and rarely used options, bringing you only the most common options based on two factors: the most plausible choices for the context or the one used most frequently in the application.

MORE INFO

A neat feature in Visual Studio
tracks the changes you make
to the source code, similar to
the Track Changes feature in
Microsoft Word. In Visual Studio,
however, whenever you modify
your code, a colored line is added
to the beginning of that line.
A yellow line indicates that a
change was made but has not
been saved yet. If the line is
green, it means the change was
saved and is now part of the code
even if you exit Visual Studio. It's
a really useful feature, and if you
want to turn it on, just click Tools,
Options, and then select the
Show All Settings check box at
the bottom left of the window. In
the tree view, expand Text Editor,
select General, and then select
Track Changes.

Figure 5-9
Getting help from IntelliSense by typing a period (.) after a valid object

Opening IntelliSense: Pressing Ctrl+Spacebar

One of the easiest ways to open the
IntelliSense window is to press
Ctrl+Spacebar. Figure 5-8 shows an example from the project currently open in my
code editor. You can see in this figure a list
of possible choices based on the context of
a form element named *Form1*.

Opening IntelliSense: Typing a Period or Left Parenthesis

Another way you can get help using
IntelliSense is by typing a period (.) after an

Figure 5-8
*You can invoke IntelliSense by hitting the Ctrl+Spacebar
keystroke combination.*

element. The IntelliSense window will show up whether you are using .NET objects or your
own objects. For example, I requested the list of possible constructs involving the variable
Form1. In this example, I was looking for the variable *TextBox1*, which represented the first
text box on our form. By typing **Me** and then a period (.)—as in **Me.**—I received the list of
all relevant objects in this context. Then by typing **t**, I received the list of all relevant components that have names beginning with that letter. I just had to scroll down to the item I
wanted: *TextBox1*. Figure 5-9 illustrates these steps in the code editor. Finally, I pressed the
Tab key to insert my selection, *TextBox1*, in the code.

TO USE INTELLISENSE

1. From the Toolbox, drag a button control to the form.

2. Double-click the button to open the button click event handler in the code editor. Then,
   where the cursor is blinking, press Ctrl+Spacebar. The IntelliSense window opens.

3. Type **m**, then **e**, and then a period (.).

4. Start typing **textbox1**. Before you finish the word, IntelliSense should open TextBox1.
   Press the Tab key to insert the component.

5. Type a period (**.**) again, type **text**, and then press the Tab key or the spacebar. The code line should look like this one:

```
Me.TextBox1.Text
```

6. Now add the equal sign (**=**), and type the string literal **"Hello, World"**; in the end, the line should look like this:

```
Me.TextBox1.Text = "Hello, World"
```

You can now build and execute the application by pressing F5 and verify that it works. When you click the button you created, you should get the string "Hello, World" in TextBox1, which ordinarily should be the first one of the three text boxes.

You can also get additional help from IntelliSense if there's more than one available choice for your situation. Typing a left parenthesis displays a list of all possible choices. For instance, when we created the console application in Chapter 3, we wrote to the console using the *Console.WriteLine* method. We used this method with a string argument, but you can do more with *Console.WriteLine* than just use a string as an argument. IntelliSense will indicate whether there is more than one option. For *Console.WriteLine*, IntelliSense indicates there are 18 possible variations, as you can see in Figure 5-10. I was looking for the second variation, which is a Boolean argument. Now it's your turn to try it.

TO SELECT FROM A LIST OF OPTIONS IN INTELLISENSE

1. If the source code is not visible, click the tab at the top of the code editor where you see the filename Form1.vb. Add a new line in the *Button1_Click* event, type **MessageBox.Show**, and then type **(**. The IntelliSense window opens and shows there are 21 possible variations for *MessageBox.Show*.

2. Press the Esc key, and then scroll through the list of options using the up and down arrows on your keyboard. Display the option identified by "15 of 21."

3. Complete the following line of code so it looks like this:

```
MessageBox.Show("Hello Again")
```

TIP

Know that at any time you're using IntelliSense, you can press the Tab key to move quickly through the selections IntelliSense presents if the item you're looking for is already selected.

NOTE

If you drop a group of controls onto a form, Visual Basic increments the number at the end of the control name, for example TextBox1, TextBox2, TextBox3, and so on.

```
Private Sub Button1_Click(ByVal s
    Console.WriteLine(|
End  ▲2 of 18▼  WriteLine (value As Boolean)
Clas value: The value to write.
```

Figure 5-10
IntelliSense lists all the possible variations of using the WriteLine *method.*

TIP

Before you can use the keyboard to scroll, you might need to press Esc to remove the contextual IntelliSense window. It's not always necessary to press Esc in these situations, but you do need to do so with *MessageBox.Show*.

NOTE

It is important to note that regardless of your current sticky tab selection, IntelliSense will always switch in real time to provide the best match for what you are typing.

4. Build and execute the application. When you click the button, you should see the "Hello, World" string in TextBox1, and then a dialog box should show up with the message "Hello Again."

Using IntelliSense Code Snippets: The Time-Saver

Code snippets are the final IntelliSense feature I'll discuss. *Code snippets* are reusable pieces of code with which you can complete a wide range of tasks without typing a single line of code. More than 200 code snippets are available in Visual Basic 2008 Express Edition. They are categorized by function and cover a wide variety of tasks:

■ Using common programming structures such as exceptions, *Try-Catch* blocks, and so forth (you'll see more about these later in this chapter)

■ Sending e-mail messages

■ Resizing a form

■ Using Visual Basic language elements such as *If*, *For*, and *While* statements with the correct syntax

MORE INFO

See the "Finding Additional Information" section later in this chapter for more information about code snippets.

Figure 5-11 shows a glimpse of a code snippet's first-level menu choices. All code snippets are made with customizable fields, which means they contain fields that are replaceable with code elements from your own applications. Going forward, you will be able to download additional code snippets from various sources such as the MSDN Web site, online communities, and other .NET vendors. You will also be able to add your own code snippets to the code snippets library to fulfill your needs in other projects.

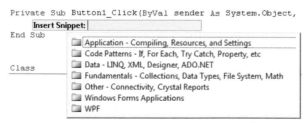

Figure 5-11
IntelliSense code snippets menus

Invoking IntelliSense Code Snippets

You can invoke code snippets in the code editor in two ways: by right-clicking and selecting Insert Snippets or by typing a question mark (**?**) in the editor and then hitting the Tab key.

TO USE CODE SNIPPETS

1. Using the previous test project, return to the code editor in the *Button1_Click* event, and call up the IntelliSense code snippets menu by using either method described earlier.

2. On the first-level menu, double-click Code Patterns: If, For Each, Try Catch, Property, Etc.; double-click Conditionals and Loops; and then select For...Next Statement. Look at Figure 5-12 to get a feel for which menu choices you should have on your screen. Double-click For...Next Statement to insert the code in the code editor.

Figure 5-12
Code snippets within the Visual Basic language menus

3. Once you select the For...Next Statement option, a generic template for that language construct appears, as shown in Figure 5-13. The highlighted fields in the "before" version (the one shown on the left of Figure 5-13) are replacement fields prepopulated with some default values that you can modify. Before you go to the next step, edit the code to match the "after" version (the one on the right of Figure 5-13).

Figure 5-13
"Before" (left) and "after" (right) example of the For...Next code snippets

If you know you want to use a *For* loop, you can also get the same snippet simply by entering **For** and then hitting the Tab key twice. You'll get the same behavior as with the other two methods explained in this section. In fact, IntelliSense will tell you how to do it. Refer to Figure 5-14 for an example.

NOTE

If you've used Visual Basic 2005 Express Edition or any other version of Visual Studio 2005, you'll remember that the green highlights in snippets stuck around the code after you were done with a snippet. In Visual Basic 2008 Express Edition, they go away as soon as you start typing something else. If you want to use the snippet functionality, simply right-click and select Show Snippet Highlighting, and you'll get the green highlights for all the snippets in that file. Note that if you close the file, this functionality is not available anymore.

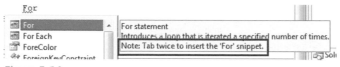

Figure 5-14
Hitting the Tab key twice to get the same snippet

4. Build and execute your application by pressing F5, and then click the button on the displayed form to execute the code snippet you've just inserted. In the second text box, you should see the numbers 1 through 10 separated by commas. This output is the result of the *For...Next* statement looping 10 times, adding the index value and a comma to the text box with each loop. In this sample, the index is *i*.

Exploring Real-Time Error Detection and Correction

We all learn differently and at different speeds. We also might make mistakes when we are learning something new, especially when we write code! So, Visual Basic 2008 gives you real-time compiler feedback and suggests corrective actions to fix mistakes. In a sense, the Visual Basic compiler is always working in the background while you are coding. Whenever you make a mistake, you'll see a blue squiggle under the faulty code. Or, if the code is not necessarily wrong but there is a potential problem, you'll see a green squiggle under the code. If you move your mouse pointer over the squiggle, a tooltip will appear to indicate why the compiler rejected your code. In some cases, a Smart Tag will appear under the last letter of the faulty code. The Smart Tag here looks a little different from other instances and is represented by a small yellow line surrounded by a red box: :ad|

If you move the mouse pointer, an exclamation point in a red circle will appear:

This indicates Visual Basic has found a potential fix for your problem. Click the down arrow next to the exclamation point, and you'll be presented with one or more potential fixes for your problem. Let's try it with our test project.

```
Private Sub But Type 'Integr' is not defined. sender As System.Object,
    Dim foo As Integr
                    1 ▾
    Me.TextBox1.Text = "Hello World"
    MessageBox.Sho Error Correction Options (Shift+Alt+F10)
```

TO USE REAL-TIME ERROR DETECTION

1. In the *Button1_Click* event, add the following line of code:

```
Dim foo as Integr
```

2. Press Enter; Visual Basic indicates there's a problem with the word *Integr* by showing a blue squiggle. Move your mouse pointer over the Smart Tag.

3. When you see the exclamation point in a red circle, click the down arrow.

4. As you can see in Figure 5-15, you're presented with a list of potential fixes for the error. Of course, the list of potential fixes is based on your current context. The error correction feature will always try to find the best solution. Select Change Integr to Integer.

5. The blue squiggle disappears, and a green squiggle appears under the variable name *foo*. Again, move your mouse pointer over the word that has the squiggle. A Smart Tag warns that the local variable *foo* is not used anywhere else in the application. Warnings are not critical and won't stop the application from executing, so you can ignore this warning.

```
Dim Foo As Integr
For i As Integ  1 ▾  1 To 10
    Me.TextBox    Type 'Integr' is not defined.
Next
                 Change 'Integr' to 'Integer'.
Sub
                 Change 'Integr' to 'UInteger'.

                 Change 'Integr' to 'IntPtr'.
```

Figure 5-15
List of potential fixes for the current error

You've just seen one case where the real-time error correction can intervene, but it can intervene on many other occasions. Identifying the errors with the background compiler is easy because it is automatic. Sometimes, the hard part is knowing what to do with errors. The error correction feature also helps you with this by showing you more than one option to fix the problem, as shown earlier in the integer example. Now let's look at a different example.

TO CHOOSE FROM SEVERAL CORRECTION OPTIONS

1. Add the following line of code in the *Button1_Click* event code:

```
ReadOnly bar As Double
```

If you have trouble typing this line of code, press Esc after typing **ReadOnly** to dismiss IntelliSense. Press Enter, and a blue squiggle appears under *ReadOnly*.

2. Move your mouse pointer over the Smart Tag. It indicates that *ReadOnly* is not valid on a local variable declaration.

3. Click the down arrow to the right of the exclamation point. Visual Basic suggests a fix and illustrates the correction by striking out the incorrect code and inserting the correct code, as shown in Figure 5-16. In this case, you want to accept the change if it makes sense in your application. If you want to accept the change, just click the blue suggestion.

Figure 5-16
Code autocorrection example

Oh, My...*My* Is Great

So far, you've seen quite a few nice features that are part of Visual Basic 2008 Express Edition. What you've not yet seen and explored is the enormous number of classes found in the .NET Framework. The .NET Framework is vast, and sometimes finding good classes and methods to solve a problem is difficult. Keeping the same productivity goal in mind, the Visual Basic team decided they had to assemble the most common classes from the .NET Framework in one collection. They decided to create this collection in a task-oriented way so that programmers can use it to accomplish the most common programming tasks. Furthermore, they decided that to provide easy access to those classes, they would create a new namespace and wrap those common classes and methods into a new set of categorized classes called the *My* namespace. Basically, the *My* namespace gives a programmer access to two different areas: .NET Framework classes and parts of a project (such as the forms, the application settings and resources, and so forth). Let's look at the list of high-level classes found in the *My* namespace:

- *Application*
- *Computer*
- *Forms*
- *Resources*
- *Settings*
- *User*
- *WebServices*

Figure 5-17 is a visual representation of these high-level classes from the code editor. In the code editor, you simply have to type the keyword **My** followed by a period (**.**) to gain access to the *My* namespace.

For instance, now you can play a .wav file simply by using the following syntax:

```
My.Computer.Audio.Play("c:\windows\media\Windows Startup.wav")
```

Test the previous line of code in the *Button1_Click* event to play the Windows start-up sound. Then build your application and execute it. It's that easy! It's intuitive and a lot easier to code now. Before the existence of the *My* namespace, to get the same functionality you would have had to use either Win32 APIs or Direct Sound from the Microsoft DirectX family and enter many more lines of code.

For more complicated tasks such as detecting network connectivity, application events, and so forth, you gain a lot of productivity using the *My* namespace. Before, you would have had to write nearly 200 lines of raw .NET Framework code—and maybe more! Now you simply have to find the construct in the *My* namespace, select it, and add the context of your application. For easier tasks, you might not save a lot of lines of code using the *My* namespace, but you certainly save time otherwise spent researching corresponding classes in the .NET Framework.

Figure 5-17
Visual representation of the first-level menu for the My *namespace*

CAUTION
If you are not using the Windows Vista or Windows XP operating system, do a search to find a .wav file on your hard disk, and then enter the path as the argument to the line of code shown earlier.

MORE INFO
You can extend the *My* namespace and classes to add your own methods. They'll also show up in IntelliSense. See the "Finding Additional Information" section later in this chapter for a link to an MSDN white paper that explains in detail how to do this.

Here are just a few of the common tasks you can expect to find in the *My* namespace:

- Displaying an application splash screen
- Getting your computer name
- Getting network settings
- Verifying that a Web site is up and running
- Reading a text file into a string
- Sending something to print on the default printer
- Getting application settings

Of course, the *My* namespace is not the answer to all problems. It's a great solution for a number of common scenarios, but to solve some other problems, you might have to call the different classes from the .NET Framework directly and write more lines of code.

Renaming

The rename feature found in Visual Basic 2008 is quite useful. It provides you, the programmer, with an easy, automatic, and effective way of changing a symbol's name (symbols include variables, filenames, visual controls, and so on) everywhere the symbol is referenced in the code. You can update the variables, controls, and any other items in your applications to meaningful names by using the renaming symbol functionality.

MORE INFO

Here is a list of what can be referenced as a symbol:
- **Type definitions such as classes, modules, structures, enums, delegates, and interfaces**
- **Type members such as methods, properties, and events**
- **Member variables of classes, modules, structures, and enums**
- **Local variables inside functions and properties**

Why Should You Rename?

So far in the test project we've worked in, we haven't paid attention to the controls' names because we didn't have to write much code and because the project was a quick prototype to test new features. At this point, our controls are all named something like Textbox1, Textbox2, Label1, and so on. That's OK for what we've been doing, but when you develop your own applications, you'll always want to give meaningful names to your controls and variables so that your code becomes self-documented and easier to read and maintain.

How to Use the Rename Feature

You can use the renaming feature from three different places within the IDE: in the Properties window, in the code, and in Solution Explorer.

The first place you can use the renaming feature is in the Properties window at design time. So far in our test project, we've used the form name *Form1*. In the next exercise, we'll rename *Form1* to *TestProjectForm*. The expectation is that this change gets propagated throughout the code in the project. But just to see how the functionality works, we'll look into all files where the *Form1* symbol is used.

TO USE THE RENAME FEATURE

1. In Solution Explorer, click the Show All Files button.

   You should see a lot of new elements showing up in the project. In the following step we'll examine the code that Visual Basic 2008 Express Edition automatically generates when we manipulate controls on the design surface.

2. Expand Form1.vb. Figure 5-18 shows what you should see in Solution Explorer. Right-click the file named Form1.Designer. vb, and then select View Code.

3. Now I'll introduce you to a useful feature: search. With the Form1.Designer.vb source code in the code editor, press Ctrl+F, and then type **Form1** in the Find What text box. Before you click the Find Next button, make sure to select Current Project from the Look In list box.

Figure 5-18
Getting to the autogenerated code for the form elements

Behind the Scenes

This is a good point to introduce a new button in the Solution Explorer toolbar. The Show All Files button looks like this in the toolbar:

In Visual Basic 2008, and especially in Express Edition, the design philosophy has always been productivity. Therefore, the Solution Explorer interface is not filled with files and settings that most users will not need on a daily basis. But some elements are included in the interface for learning purposes or for when you are solving complex problems and might want to directly dig into all the files associated with your project. Some files are generated automatically when you perform actions in the IDE, and in most situations it's just fine like that; you do not need to care about all the details all the time. In situations where you want more control, you can click the Show All Files button and go directly to the component of your choice.

OOP Terminology

Although this book is not an OOP book, we'll certainly use many of those constructs in the applications that we build. I talked about OOP in Chapter 1, "Introducing Microsoft Visual Basic 2008 Express Edition," and in Chapter 4, but if you want to learn more about this paradigm, you can go to the Start Page. If it's not visible, just click View, Other Windows, and then select Start Page. On the Start Page, click the Learn VB hyperlink in the Getting Started section. Locate the Programming with Objects: Using Classes section. Then click and read whenever you want to learn more about OOP and the Visual Basic language.

Figure 5-19 shows how the search should be configured.

4. Search for all occurrences of *Form1* in the code by clicking the Find Next button. You should see that the search goes through four files: Form1.vb, Form1.Designer.vb, Application.Designer.vb, and Application.myapp.

   Once all instances of *Form1* have been found, a dialog box will display a message saying that the search is complete and that there are no more occurrences left based on your search criteria.

Figure 5-19
The Find and Replace dialog box

5. Now that all instances of *Form1* have been identified, you can rename the form. To do that, select the Form1.vb [Design] tab to return to the designer surface. Then click the title bar to select the form.

6. In the Properties window, be sure the form control named *Form1* is selected. Modify the *(Name)* property by changing *Form1* to *TestProjectForm*. Press Enter to begin renaming. A small hourglass appears while the renaming is in process.

7. Now repeat the search from steps 3 and 4, and you'll see that the only occurrence left is a string that corresponds to the Form control's *Text* property (that is, the title bar name).

8. You can also rename a symbol directly in the code. In Form1.vb, place the cursor anywhere in the word *TextBox1* in the following line of code:

```
Me.TextBox1.Text = "Hello, World"
```

9. Right-click, and select Rename; a dialog box like the one on the left of Figure 5-20 appears. Replace *TextBox1* with *tbMessage*; the dialog box should now look like the one on the right of Figure 5-20.

10. Click OK to replace all occurrences of *TextBox1* with *tbMessage*.

    A search should find only one comment and the *Name* property of the text box control with the string "TextBox1"—it's that easy. Imagine how much time you would save using the rename feature if you had 10 files with hundreds of lines of code. Not only would you be sure to find every occurrence, but the code would be a lot easier to read.

Figure 5-20
Rename dialog boxes: before (left) and after (right) a rename

11. The third way to rename a symbol, and in this case only for project elements, is to do it directly in Solution Explorer. Even though earlier we changed the *Form1* variable into something more meaningful, the filename Form1 hasn't changed because it's not in the source code; it's in Solution Explorer and contained in the project, so it's still Form1.vb. For consistency, right-click the filename Form1.vb in Solution Explorer, select Rename, and then change the filename to TestProjectFormOtherName.vb. Two things will happen: first, you'll see that the filename and all dependent filenames are automatically changed to the new name; and second, you'll see that all references to *TestProjectForm* are now changed to *TestProjectFormOtherName*. You can verify this renaming change by pressing Ctrl+F and performing a search on the old name (Form1.vb).

Exploring Common Windows Controls

I will not spend a lot of time here explaining all the details and properties of each control in the Toolbox. This book is not a reference about Windows Forms programming. Other books do a great job with that topic. However, Table 5-1 provides a quick introduction to the common controls you will find in most Windows applications.

Visual Representation	Name	Description
Button1	Button	The button control lets a user communicate a decision or initiate an action. In your application, a button clicked by the user triggers an event that your code needs to handle.
	TextBox	The text box is used to get user input. On the screen it can be a single or multiline control. It can also provide password character masking if you need this behavior in your application. It's a good choice for user input that is not restrictive in choices, such as a Boolean decision (yes/no or on/off) or a list of specific choices (like a list of country names). It's good for names, addresses, phone numbers, URLs, and so on.
Label1	Label	The label is usually simple text used to describe other controls. It is generally not an interactive control.
○ Grayscale ○ Color	RadioButton	This control is used when multiple choices are offered but the user can pick only one from the list. Let's say you have an application and you want to provide the option to print in grayscale or color. You could use two radio buttons so that the user can select the desired method.

Table 5-1
Common Controls

Visual Representation	Name	Description
☐ AC ☐ CD Changer ☐ Metallic Paint ☐ ABS	CheckBox	A check box is great for Boolean choices (for example, on/off, yes/no, and so on). It can also be used in a group of check boxes to indicate characteristics of a single entity. For instance, in a car-ordering tool that is part of a dealership application, you could have check boxes for all the car characteristics (that is, AM/FM radio, CD changer, heated seats, metallic paint, and so on).
[▼] [▼] Alabama Arkansas California Connecticut Washington	ComboBox	A combo box is a combination of a text box and a drop-down list with valid choices. It's great for displaying an editable text box with a list of permitted values. You can have auto-complete, and the values can be sorted. The values can come from static entry or from other sources of data such as a database. For instance, a good example is selecting a state. You can either enter the state name or select it from the list of possible values.
Joe John Brad Mark Jim Joe John Brad Mark Jim	ListBox	A list box is a short list of valid choices for the domain this component represents. This control is great when there is a list of possible choices that is not too big in number. It does not allow the user to enter text but lets the user select one or more than one choice by using Ctrl or Shift.

Table 5-1 (continued)
Common Controls

Visual Representation	Name	Description
Name [_____] Customer Name	ToolTip	The tooltip control is helpful for displaying information about a control when a user holds the mouse pointer over the control.
1971 [⬍]	NumericUpDown	This control is really useful when you want the user to select a numerical value in a defined set of numbers. It allows the user to select a single numerical value from the list using the up or down button to increment and decrement the number. It's a perfect way to force the user to pick a numerical value for the year component of a date.

Table 5-1 (continued)
Common Controls

Many more controls exist than those shown here, but this table should make it clear that you have a plethora of controls available to perform many tasks. To save time and effort, you can usually find a control to provide the results you want with very little effort. It is especially desirable if the control you pick can restrict choices or how the data is selected without having to perform any other validation. In software development, always keep the 80/20 rule in mind: 80 percent of results for 20 percent effort. Keep it simple; you don't need to reinvent the wheel.

What Happens When an Event Is Triggered?

All Windows applications are event-driven. This means that whenever you select a menu item, click a button, or even move from one text box to another, you are generating an event. Blocks of code attached to each of your actions execute as you work. Events are generated not only by your actions but also by the surrounding environment, namely, Windows or external sources. To understand what "external sources" means, think about any Instant messenger application, for example, Windows Live Messenger. When you chat with someone and exchange data back and forth, you are actually generating events. In nontechnical terms, data coming from your friend over the Internet is an *event*.

These events exist for a multitude of actions you often take—probably without even realizing they are events. Some events are handled for you by autogenerated code, such as clicking the red X in the right corner of an application, and some others need to be handled by your code.

In this section, we'll start to work on wiring source code to events. For practice, we will wire two objects from our test project. Before beginning, use what you've learned so far to make the test project look like Figure 5-21.

When an event is triggered, the code that is wired to handle the event is executed. If there is no code attached to a particular event, nothing happens. Our application is basically in that stage right now (except for the button that was doing some work for us, as shown previously). We will add some functionality to our test project application by wiring the Save menu item and the toolbar Save button to source code that will save all the content of the text boxes to a simple text file in the current directory. Because the Save and Open file dialog boxes are standard (and also to get a consistent feel to applications), the Visual Basic development team decided to write save and open controls and make them available to you. We'll take advantage of this shortcut in our exercise.

Figure 5-21
Customer Info form

NOTE

To add the menus and toolbar buttons, go to the Toolbox in the Menus & Toolbars category, and add a MenuStrip control and a ToolStrip control to the form. Next, select each control, open the Smart Tag menu, and select Insert Standard Items.

TO WIRE SOURCE CODE TO EVENTS

1. Drag the SaveFileDialog control in the Toolbox's Dialogs category to the form. This control has no design-time representation; it will appear (along with the MenuStrip and

TIP

If you want to look at all the possible events that can be fired for a particular control, you can click the yellow lightning icon at the top of the Properties window. To return to the properties, you just have to click the little sheet symbol to the left of the yellow lightning icon.

Using Comments in Your Code

One good habit you should start embracing when writing code is to comment your code. Right now, the code for the problems we are solving isn't too complicated. But keep in mind that adding comments serves the following purposes: first, your code becomes much more maintainable because you can return six months later and, if the comments are good, be able to understand what you developed. It also makes your code more readable and facilitates getting help from somebody. Write your comments in regular English without too much jargon. Comments are never compiled in the application you execute, so they will never slow down the performance of your application.

Using Comments in Your Code (continued)

ToolStrip controls) only in the component tray, which is the gray section below the designer surface. See Figure 5-22 for the location of the SaveFileDialog control.

We'll use the SaveFileDialog control to wire the click event to both the Save button on the toolbar and the Save item in the File menu. To have the same operation performed when either event occurs, we'll write a block of code called a *method,* and we will then call this method in all places we need it. The block of code will perform the same operation whether it is triggered by the button on the toolbar or by the menu selection.

2. Click the blue disk icon on the ToolStrip control to select it. Refer to the Properties window to be sure you have the correct control, which should be called SaveToolStripButton, as shown in Figure 5-23.

Figure 5-22
Design-time representation of the SaveFileDialog control

Figure 5-23
Verify that the name and type of control is the one you intend to work with.

3. Double-click the blue disk on the designer surface, and you will be presented with the default event template for this control, which is the click event.

4. Add the following line of code to the *SaveToolStripButton_Click* event procedure. (I will explain what it does in a moment.)

```
Me.SaveFileDialog1.ShowDialog()
```

log1 dialog box by calling the *ShowDialog()* method on it. At this point, if you want to see the effect of the change, just build and execute the application by pressing F5, and then click the Save button to see that the Save dialog box does appear.

6. In every SaveFileDialog dialog box, there is a Save button and a Cancel button. The Cancel button is automatically taken care of for us. But we need to wire what is going to happen when the user clicks the Save button of that new dialog box.

7. Make sure you have stopped the execution of the application. Now, to wire the Save button, select the saveFileDialog1 icon in the component tray, and double-click it to get to the most common event, which is the *FileOk* event in this case.

8. We'll use code snippets to insert the code that will execute when the user clicks the Save button. Remember that to get to the code snippets, you need to right-click in the code editor, select Insert Snippet, and then follow the different path choices. You need to write to a file, so use the following path: Application – Compiling, Resources, and Settings: Write to a Text File. When you are finished, your code should look like the "SaveFileDia-log1_FileOk Method" listing shown here. Examine the comments to understand what we are trying to accomplish.

> **TIP**
>
> **Some lines of code can get rather long. In Visual Basic you can use a space and an underscore (_) to indicate that a line of code continues on the next line. A line of code can typically be broken where a space occurs; however, in some locations (such as within a quoted string), a line cannot be broken.**

SaveFileDialog1_FileOk Method

```
Private Sub SaveFileDialog1_FileOk(ByVal sender As System.Object, ByVal e As _
    System.ComponentModel.CancelEventArgs) Handles SaveFileDialog1.FileOk
    Try
        ' The property FileName from the first argument in WriteAllText refers
        ' to the filename selected by the user in SaveFileDialog1
        ' Then we are passing the content of each TextBox and concatenating the
        ' Carriage Return-Line Feed constant
        ' The last parameter indicates whether we should append to a file if it
        ' exists. False will not, and therefore it will re-create the file each
        ' time. In order to add the content of the first box, we need to put
        ' true for the 2nd and 3rd  write; otherwise, only the last write would
        ' be there if they are all false.
        My.Computer.FileSystem.WriteAllText(Me.SaveFileDialog1.FileName, _
```

As you can see in the listing in step 8, you can comment your code by inserting a single quotation mark and then typing your comment. Your comment should appear in green; if not, then your line is not seen as a comment by the compiler. Another good way to comment your code is to use two buttons from one of the toolbars. Let's say you decide that all the previous code in the FileOk event is not the code you want to execute because you want to test something else. You do not want to delete all the text, but you can comment out the code by selecting it and then clicking the Comment Out the Selected Lines button. And if you want to uncomment a block of code, you just have to select the code you want to uncomment and then click the Uncomment the Selected Lines button.

5. This block of code displays the SaveFileDia-

the metadata, shortcut, replacement variables, and replacement assemblies. Here is the link to that tool: http://msdn2.microsoft.com/en-us/vbasic/bb973770.aspx. *The videos from MSDN are another good source of information. I suggest you watch the following two lessons (even though they were made for Visual Basic 2005, they still apply); they will reinforce a lot of topics covered in this chapter:*

Lesson 2 video: http://msdn2.microsoft.com/en-us/beginner/bb308740.aspx

Lesson 3 video: http://msdn2.microsoft.com/en-us/beginner/bb308743.aspx

Those two lessons are a pretty good complement to this chapter. As an advanced topic, if you want to extend the My *namespace, here is a good MSDN white paper:*

http://www.msdn.microsoft.com/msdnmag/issues/05/07/my/default.aspx

Wow, this was a big chapter that covered a lot of features. These features will definitely help you write applications on your own. Specifically, the chapter covered IDE features such as snap

```
                        Me.tbMessage.Text & vbCrLf, False)
            My.Computer.FileSystem.WriteAllText(Me.SaveFileDialog1.FileName, _
                Me.TextBox2.Text & vbCrLf, True)
            My.Computer.FileSystem.WriteAllText(Me.SaveFileDialog1.FileName, _
                Me.TextBox3.Text & vbCrLf, True)
        Catch fileException As ApplicationException
            Throw fileException
        End Try
    End Sub
```

9. Now we just need to attach the same event code to the File, Save menu selection. Double-click the Save choice in the File menu, and add the same code as in step 4. Build the application, and execute it by pressing F5. Type some text in the text boxes, and then save the content to a file by using the Save menu or the Save toolbar button. You should verify that the content of the file your application saved is really what was on the form. So, to verify that it worked properly, open the file with Visual Studio by clicking File, Open File and then browsing to the location of the saved file. Open it to view its contents.

You just handled two events, but I want to point out that you already handled events previously by coding the *Button1_Click* event and modifying properties of other controls. For instance, you modified the *Text* property of the text box controls when you handled the button click. And you were able to do that by using the control's *Name* property.

Finding Additional Information

With the code snippet editor you can create, edit, and debug your own code snippets. You can also fill all

In Summary...

lines to help you to align the controls on the form. It also covered the rich features of Intelli-Sense, which help you type your code by either suggesting appropriate choices, completing code sentences for you, or providing you with code snippets. In the end, IntelliSense is there to reduce the amount of typing you do, to help you learn the language, and to help you increase your productivity. On top of that, it is a great feature for beginners.

You then saw how the compiler is working in the background in real time to detect errors and provide you with suggestions to fix them. The chapter also reviewed the introduction of the *My* namespace in Visual Basic. This new namespace provides an easy way to perform a multitude of common tasks by encapsulating a lot of lines of .NET raw code in simpler, one-line syntax. Often, one line of code replaces up to 200 lines of raw .NET code.

You then saw the benefits of the renaming feature to replace symbol names in all project files. It is especially useful to replace autogenerated variable names with more meaningful variable names. You examined the most common controls you will find in every Windows application with some graphical examples and learned when to use them. Finally, the chapter ended with how event-based programming is performed.

In the next chapter, you'll put into practice everything you just learned in this chapter. You'll also take a look at some new features, controls, and concepts that you'll use as we continue with the Web browser project.

Chapter 6

Modifying Your Web Browser

After learning about the avalanche of new concepts presented in the first few chapters, you're now ready to apply your skills and take your Web browser to the next level. In this chapter, you'll add rich features to your browser such as a splash screen, an About dialog box, tool strips, menu strips, a tool strip container that will give you a rich user experience à la Windows Internet Explorer, a status strip, a progress bar, and professional-looking toolbars with "déjà vu" icons. You'll also learn about new Microsoft Visual Basic 2008 IDE features such as the Document Outline window. You'll also learn to respond to events coming from the WebBrowser control. Finally, you'll learn about Windows Presentation Foundation, because you will modify your Web browser project using this new technology.

When you load an application, you often see something called a *splash screen*. Some good examples of splash screens are the opening information boxes you see for Microsoft Office and Visual Studio 2008. Although the splash screens are often very nice looking, they aren't there just to display the software version and some appealing artwork or just to make sure you're not bored. These screens serve a function. Once you've started an application, a lot of processing is happening; for instance, the application is connecting to databases, populating controls with data from the database, getting saved configurations for user interface (UI) preferences, and so on. Displaying the splash screen while all of this processing is happening helps inform the user that the application is indeed working.

Technically speaking, a splash screen is a Windows form that does not allow any input from the user. It usually has a nice presentation form with some artwork, the application name, its version, and often some legal text. One of the first features you'll add to your Web browser application is a splash screen.

In this chapter, you'll modify the browser application you created in Chapter 4, "Creating Your Own Web Browser in Less Than Five Minutes." If you installed the companion content to the default location, you can find the application at the following location on your hard disk: Documents\Microsoft Press\VB 2008 Express\Chapter6\. Look for a folder named Start in the Chapter6 folder. Double-click the MyOwnBrowser.sln solution. If you want, you can also start from your own Chapter 4 browser project.

TO CREATE A SPLASH SCREEN

1. Open the Add New Item dialog box. You can do this either by clicking Project, Add Windows Form or by going to Solution Explorer, right-clicking the project name (in this case, MyOwnBrowser), selecting Add, and then selecting Windows Form. The Add New Item dialog box appears, and you will see that a Splash Screen template already exists.

2. Select the Splash Screen template, and name it Splash.vb, as shown in Figure 6-1. Then click Add.

Figure 6-1
Adding a new Windows form: New Item template choices

3. Go to the Design view of the splash screen, and you'll see that the screen is split into multiple squares. In fact, the splash screen is a TableLayoutPanel control. This control helps you by arranging the layout of your components in a table format with a set of rows and columns. You can customize the rows and columns by modifying properties in the Properties window or by using source code. The control also features a Smart Tag to easily add or remove rows and columns. (The splash screen has two rows and two columns by default.) If you look carefully, you'll see that the Splash Screen template has another TableLayoutPanel control located in the bottom-right cell (represented by the dotted rectangle).

Figure 6-2
Use the Properties window to find all the controls on a selected form

NOTE

Each cell in a TableLayoutPanel control can contain only one control, but you can always insert another TableLayoutPanel control as was done for the Splash Screen template.

TIP

Often, it's difficult to select a particular control. To see all controls in the currently displayed form, you first have to click anywhere on the form, and then you can select from the drop-down list at the top of the Properties window. Figure 6-2 shows the drop-down list for the splash screen form. To select any particular control, highlight it in the list, which will select it on the design surface.

The application title, version, and copyright information are all obtained dynamically. This means the form will get the values from a variable or a setting somewhere in your project. In fact, at run time those three pieces of information are obtained when the splash screen is loaded by looking up application settings stored in the Project Designer's Application pane.

TO VIEW THE APPLICATION TITLE, VERSION, AND COPYRIGHT PROPERTIES

1. Select MyOwnBrowser in Solution Explorer, right-click, and choose Properties.

   The Project Designer page opens. The Project Designer page has a series of information tabs (as shown in Figure 6-3). You'll work mainly on the first tab for now, which is the Application pane. You'll configure several elements on this pane. All the elements you'll modify will affect how the application looks.

Figure 6-3
Project Designer page

2. To change the application icon, click the Icon drop-down list, and select <Browse...>. Find the Chapter6 directory where you installed the book's sample files and look for the globe.ico file in the Images folder. (If you installed the companion content at the default location, then the file should be at the following location on your hard disk: Documents\Microsoft Press\VB 2008 Express\Chapter6\Complete\Images.)

You've changed the icon of your application assembly; in other words, you've changed the icon of the executable binary (.exe) file itself. If you build the application and look on your hard disk where the application is compiled (as you learned in a previous chapter, all your projects are by default located at a path such as Documents\Visual Studio 2008\Projects\MyOwnBrowser\MyOwnBrowser\bin\Debug or \bin\Release), you'll find that your application, MyOwnBrowser.exe, has the globe icon that you've just selected instead of a default icon.

3. Click the Assembly Information button. You should see a dialog box that looks like the one in Figure 6-4.

NOTE
You're not changing the icon of the main form when doing this application icon change. To do that, you need to change the form icon's property by assigning a bitmap image. You'll change the main form icon later in this chapter.

NOTE
The assembly version information you see here is also what the application will display in the splash screen you're creating. You'll see the source code that will display the information on the splash screen later in the chapter.

Figure 6-4
Assembly Information dialog box

In the Project Designer, when the Enable XP Visual Styles check box is selected, your application will inherit the look and feel of Microsoft Windows XP. For example, it gives you controls with rounded corners that light up when you hold your mouse pointer over them. There's also a new colorful progress bar and many other features you've probably seen before. Note that when executed on a platform that doesn't support Windows XP themes, the application reverts to the traditional Windows look and feel (Windows 2000 or Windows 98). As mentioned, later in this chapter we will develop the application using WPF, and we will then have an application with the visual styles of the Windows Vista operating system.

4. Change the Copyright text box by replacing the word *Microsoft* with your name, and keep the rest of the information as it is. (If the Copyright text box is not already filled with your information, change it to match your name or company information.)

5. Insert spaces between the words *MyOwnBrowser* in the Title text box. (This string is used to display the application title on the splash screen.) Insert two spaces to get the following title: My Own Browser.

6. Click OK to close the Assembly Information dialog box.

7. To attach the splash screen to your application, select Splash from the Splash Screen drop-down list at the bottom of the Project Designer's Application tab.

8. Save the application (pressing Ctrl+Shift+S saves all the files, and pressing Ctrl+S saves the current file), and press F5 to run it.

You should see the splash screen for about two seconds before the browser form appears. Two seconds isn't a long time, so you might not have time to really look at it. To see what it actually looks like at run time, look at Figure 6-5. The title, version number, and copyright information appear automatically. But how does the information get there?

Figure 6-5
Splash screen in action

Those three pieces of information are obtained programmatically using a familiar construct—the *My* namespace. (By "programmatically," I mean writing code to set or get something you would ordinarily set or get using a UI tool, such as the Properties window or the Project Designer.) One important part of the Splash Screen template is the *Form Load* event; each form has a *Load* event that happens just before the form is displayed. This is where you'll usually perform the initialization for controls on your form. Review the *Splash_Load* method (in Splash.vb), specifically the following highlighted code, to understand where and how the *My* classes and methods are used to populate the fields on the splash screen:

```vb
Private Sub splash_Load(ByVal sender As Object, ByVal e As System.EventArgs) _
    Handles Me.Load
    'Set up the dialog text at runtime according to the application's assembly
    'information.

    'TODO: Customize the application's assembly information in the
    'Application pane of the project properties dialog (under the Project menu).

    'Application title
    If My.Application.Info.Title <> "" Then
        ApplicationTitle.Text = My.Application.Info.Title
    Else
        'If the application title is missing, use the application name, without
        ' the extension
        ApplicationTitle.Text = System.IO.Path.GetFileNameWithoutExtension( _
            My.Application.Info.AssemblyName)
    End If

    'Format the version information using the text set into the Version
    'design time as the formatting string.  This allows for effective
    'localization if desired. Build and revision information could be included
    'by using the following code and changing the Version control's design-time
    'text to "Version {0}.{1:00}.{2}.{3}" or something similar.
    'See String.Format() in Help for more information.
    '
    '   Version.Text = System.String.Format(Version.Text, _
    '     My.Application.Info.Version.Major, My.Application.Info.Version.Minor, _
    '     My.Application.Info.Version.Build, My.Application.Info.Version.Revision)
```

```
Version.Text = System.String.Format(Version.Text, _
    My.Application.Info.Version.Major, _
    My.Application.Info.Version.Minor)

'Copyright info
Copyright.Text = My.Application.Info.Copyright
End Sub
```

As you can see, *My.Application.Info* was useful for obtaining application settings without reading those settings from a special file. That's the magic of the *My* namespace.

You might think the time the splash screen is displayed on the screen is too short. For example, a bigger application might need to open connections to databases, retrieve information, and do all kinds of initialization upon launching, so it might take more than two seconds. Or, you might simply want your users to have more time to look at the screen. There's an easy way to change the amount of time it displays. You simply have to call the *My* namespace to the rescue! To add the line of code that will change the delay, you need to open a method from the splash screen form and class:

1. Right-click Splash.vb, and select View Code.

2. Click the drop-down list on the right side of the window, and select the New method. Look at Figure 6-6 to see where you can access the list of methods for that class.

MORE INFO

You can change the bitmap image on the splash screen to whatever you want by modifying the *MainLayoutPanel – BackgroundImage* property in the Properties window. You can also change the size of the splash screen to fit the size of your image or use imaging software to change the size of the image to fit the splash screen.

Figure 6-6
List of methods for the Splash *class*

3. Just insert the two bold lines in the following code. The delay is expressed in milliseconds and in this case will display your splash screen for three and a half seconds.

```
Public Sub New()

    ' This call will change the display time for the splash screen
    My.Application.MinimumSplashScreenDisplayTime = 3500

    ' This call is required by the Windows Form Designer.
    InitializeComponent()

    ' Add any initialization after the InitializeComponent() call.

End Sub
```

MORE INFO

I'm sure you've seen the formatting in the Properties window for the version number. This special notation is how strings are formatted. To really understand, I recommend you press F1 to search the software documentation for *String.Format*. You'll find all possible formatting options and how to use them.

Interacting Through Dialog Boxes

The dialog boxes you create help the user interact with the software. They are additional forms that you add to your application. In the following sections, you'll add two dialog boxes to your Web browser: an About dialog box and a Navigate dialog box.

Adding an About Dialog Box

The first dialog box you'll add is an About dialog box, which exists in most Windows applications. This dialog box contains essentially the same information as the splash screen but sometimes contains more legal, system, and version information.

Before you add this About dialog box, you'll give Form1 a more meaningful name. (Keep in mind that everything in your application needs to be meaningful for readability and maintenance.) You'll also prepare the application for a transformation into a more feature-rich Internet browser.

NOTE

When a procedure directive tells you to add a control and then name it *XYZ*, it means you need to add the control to the design surface, go to the Properties window, and then change the *(Name)* property of the control to *XYZ*.

TIP

To delete the event handler code, in Solution Explorer, right-click the Browser.vb file, and select View Code. Delete the entire *btnGo_Click* method.

TO ADD AN ABOUT DIALOG BOX

1. In Solution Explorer, rename Form1.vb to Browser.vb.

2. On the Browser form, delete the *txtURL* and *btnGo* controls. Delete the *btnGo_Click* event handler by removing its signature and content from the Browser.vb file.

3. On the Browser form, select the WebBrowser control, and using the Smart Tag, select Dock in Parent Container.

4. As you did for the splash screen, add a new item to your project, but this time when presented with the templates, choose the About Box template. Then name it AboutBox.vb.

Similar to the splash screen, the About dialog box will be populated with information from the project settings in the Project Designer window. At this point, if you run the application, there is no link between your About dialog box and the rest of your browser, so it won't show up anywhere. Usually, the About dialog box shows up when you request it from the Help menu, so you'll add this missing link now.

TO LINK THE ABOUT BOX TO THE HELP MENU

1. Select the Browser.vb [Design]* tab to return to the Browser form's Design view. Drag a MenuStrip control from the Toolbox to the design surface to add it to the Browser form. Name it *msBrowser*.

2. To add the Help menu, select the menu strip on the form, click the Smart Tag, and then select Insert Standard Items. You'll get a familiar Windows application menu strip and its menu choices with their submenus, icons, and keyboard shortcuts.

3. Delete all menu choices except the Help menu and the About command in the Help menu. To perform this cleanup, select any menu choice, right-click to open the context menu, and select Delete to remove it. Also remove the menu separators (that is, the lines separating menu choices).

4. To wire the new About form to the About... menu choice, double-click the About... menu choice to get to the *AboutToolStripMenuItem_Click* event handler.

5. Add the following line of code to the event handler:

```
AboutBox.ShowDialog()
```

6. Save the application, and then run it. Select Help, About…. The screen should resemble Figure 6-7. The *ShowDialog()* method opens the form in the middle of the executing application, and nothing else can happen until you click one of its buttons or the red X to close the dialog box. In this case, it has only the OK button.

NOTE
I modified the Assembly Information fields in the Project Designer to come up with the information displayed in the About dialog box. You can do the same. You simply add or modify the content in the Description, Company, Product, and Copyright fields.

Figure 6-7
About My Own Browser dialog box showing up in your newly refined browser application

You're probably wondering why the application worked when you clicked the OK button even though you didn't write any code to handle this event. This is an example of the productivity gains you'll get when using templates. The template includes the code to handle the button *Click* event. Review the source code for the dialog box by right-clicking the AboutBox.vb file in Solution Explorer and selecting View Code. Again, as covered earlier,

MORE INFO

As you saw if you watched the object-oriented tutorial movie at MSDN (go to *http://msdn2. microsoft.com/en-us/beginner/ bb308752.aspx* and look at Lesson 6, Parts 1 and 2), *Me* means the current instance of an object. In this case, this is an instance of the *AboutBox* class. *Me* is used to access all the public fields, properties, and methods defined in the class. In this example, *Me* is allowing you to assign some content to fields that belong to the *AboutBox* class, which are also the fields from the *AboutBox* form. Remember that everything in .NET is an object—fields in a form are members of a class, and a form instance is an object.

MORE INFO

A dialog box is often a *modal* form. It has a predefined behavior in which the user can't click anything other than controls on that form: the OK and Cancel buttons or the red X button to close the form. This means that until the dialog box is closed, the user won't be able to click anything else in the application. To understand what's happening here, just think about the Print dialog box in Microsoft Word: once it is displayed, you can't return to your document to make any changes while the Print dialog box is open. That's because the Print dialog box is a modal form.

using *My.Application.Info* gives you quick access to application information in the Project Designer. Also note that the *Click* event has a single line of code that tells the form to call the *Close()* method.

Now that you've added the About dialog box, it should be easy to add another that will allow your users to navigate to Web pages.

Adding a Navigate Dialog Box

Deleting the button and the address controls from our simple browser removed the ability to navigate to a Web page. This, of course, is not useful for a Web browser. Now you'll add a dialog box that will give your user another way to navigate to Web pages.

TO ADD A NAVIGATE DIALOG BOX

1. As you did for the About dialog box and the splash screen, add another new item to your project. Using the templates, select a Dialog template, and name it Navigate.vb.

2. Add a label and a text box to the dialog box:

   a. Name the label *lblInfoUrl*. Set the *Text* property to *Type an Internet address and My Own Browser will open it for you*.

   b. Name the text box *txtUrl*, set the *AutoCompleteMode* property to *SuggestAppend*, and set the *AutoCompleteSource* property to *AllUrl*.

3. Size and position the controls and the form so that the Navigate form looks like the one in Figure 6-8.

Figure 6-8
Navigate form

You've set some of the autocomplete properties of the text box to behave the same way they do in Windows Internet Explorer. This means the text box will suggest and append URLs based on the letters the user types. You'll now wire this form to the application using a new menu called Navigate.

TO WIRE THE FORM TO THE APPLICATION USING THE NAVIGATE MENU

1. Return to the Browser form in Design view, and look at the top of the Browser form. You already have a menu strip with the Help menu; now add a new menu to your menu strip by clicking beside the Help menu and typing **&Navigate**. The & in front of the N will create an underscored N so that the user can press the keystroke combination Alt+N to fire the *Click* event on the Navigate menu.

2. You'll see that the Navigate menu shows up to the right of the Help menu. To move a menu, simply select it, and drag it where you want. In this case, drop it to the left of the Help menu.

3. Before adding the code for the event itself, you need to add an important line of code. Remember that in Visual Basic everything is an object, and if you want to manipulate another form and exchange data between the two forms, you first need to create an object of that type that is visible to your main form (the Browser form)—in this case, an object of type *Navigate*. Create an instance of the Navigate form outside the source code of any event handler by writing the following line of code in Browser.vb:

```
Dim NavigateWindow As New Navigate()
```

Look at Figure 6-9 to see where to insert it.

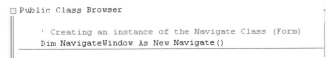

```
Public Class Browser

    ' Creating an instance of the Navigate Class (Form)
    Dim NavigateWindow As New Navigate()
```

Figure 6-9
Creating a new instance of the form Navigate

MORE INFO

It's important for you to start learning how to test your own code by doing what's known as *black box* testing. At a high level, this consists of testing what the user can do and what is presented to the user. This means you need to test every little detail in the UI as well as the situations the UI offers to the user. When you perform a task such as this, I suggest you create a spreadsheet that contains a matrix of all the test cases. Then fill it in as you test. This will give you a visual representation of all tests and features. You're now doing this manually because your application is small in scope, but you'll quickly realize that with a bigger application or an application you might sell, you'll need some sort of automated mechanism to make sure the tests are all executed and that you're not forgetting any. You'll then require a UI testing tool, and in most situations you'll need to build your own tools. But that's out of context for this book; I just wanted to emphasize the importance of testing your application.

Now that you have an instance of the *Navigate* form class, you can write code to exchange data back and forth between the two forms. And that's exactly what will happen. When the Navigate form is displayed and the user clicks the OK button with a URL in the text box, the WebBrowser control will navigate to the specified URL. Also note that the URL text box will be cleared after navigating to the URL to make sure it's empty the next time the user accesses it.

4. On the Browser form, double-click the Navigate menu to add the *NavigateToolStripMenuItem_Click* event handler.

5. Add the following code to the *NavigateToolStripMenuItem_Click* event handler:

```
If (NavigateWindow.ShowDialog() = Windows.Forms.DialogResult.OK) Then
    Me.myBrowser.Navigate(NavigateWindow.txtUrl.Text)
End If
NavigateWindow.txtUrl.Text = ""
```

6. Build and execute the application by pressing F5. The form should resemble Figure 6-10 when the user selects the Navigate menu and enters a URL.

Figure 6-10
Execution of My Own Browser using the Navigate form with auto-complete

7. Now, test the application with all the modifications you've made. Verify every new aspect:

- Does pressing Alt+N take you to the Navigate form?
- Can you hit Cancel with/without content?
- Can you navigate to a good URL/bad URL?
- Is the text box empty when you return to the Navigate form (that is, after you've performed all the other steps and pressed Alt+N)?

Having a Professional Look and Feel at Your Fingertips

In the following sections, you'll continue to add functionality to your browser using components that you might have seen in other Microsoft applications. You'll add appealing and professional touches to your application quickly and easily.

Adding a Tool Strip Container and Some Tools

A tool strip container is a new control that ships with Visual Basic 2008, and with it your users can customize your application like they customize the toolbars in Microsoft Office Outlook or Microsoft Office Word. The tool strip container has five panels, one on each side of the screen, and a content panel in the middle. You can have all of them on the screen enabled at one time or choose them selectively at design time. You can also control them with source code. You can put a tool strip and a menu strip in a tool strip container at design time, and at run time your users have the opportunity to arrange their workspace the way they like. The tool strip container gives your application the same look and feel as Outlook (see Figure 6-11). For instance, I was able to put two tool strips on the left of my screen. This means those tool strips are embedded in the tool strip container's left panel. But I could easily

Figure 6-11
Tool strip container example in Outlook

move any visible toolbar back to the top, the right, or the bottom. With a tool strip container, you give your users control of the layout of their tool strips and menu strips, which is a great feature to have.

TO ADD A TOOL STRIP CONTAINER

1. Drag a tool strip container onto the Browser form's design surface.

2. Rename *toolstripcontainer1* to *mainFormToolStripContainer*.

3. Use the Smart Tag from the tool strip container to select Dock Fill in Form.

Wait a minute...where is the WebBrowser control? Don't worry, it didn't disappear. The control's z-order has changed. The WebBrowser control is visually under the tool strip container, and its parent is not the tool strip container but the Browser form.

The Document Outline window is a valuable tool that can help you solve this problem and save you a lot of time. For those of you familiar with previous versions of Visual Studio, this view existed before but only for HTML and ASPX documents. With Visual Studio 2008, it has been extended to Windows Forms applications. To display the Document Outline window in your IDE, simply click View, Other Windows, Document Outline, or press Ctrl+Alt+T. This view lets you manage all the controls on your form. It shows how the controls are arranged on the screen and which controls belong to another control. For instance, right now you cannot see the WebBrowser control, but if you display the Document Outline window, you'll see that the WebBrowser control is at the same level as the newly added tool strip container (see Figure 6-12). To rearrange the order and change how the controls are displayed, follow the next two steps.

> **NOTE**
>
> The *z-order* is the control's position relative to the other windows or controls on the screen; think of it as the third dimension or as being on top of or beneath other controls.

Figure 6-12
The Document Outline window for the My Own Browser project

TO REARRANGE THE ORDER OF CONTROLS

1. In the Document Outline window, select the WebBrowser control called *myBrowser*, and drag it just below the tool strip container content panel called

mainFormToolStripContainer.ContentPanel. (When you drag the WebBrowser control, a black line indicates where the control will be dropped if you release the mouse button.)

2. Now display the form again. The WebBrowser control is in the middle of the form. But as you can see, the MenuStrip control is not in the tool strip container. Repeat step 1 for the MenuStrip control, but instead of dropping it in the content panel, drop it in the top panel of the tool strip container (*mainFormToolStripContainer.TopToolStripPanel*).

Now the only thing missing from the new menu strip is a dotted grip like the one shown earlier in Figure 6-11. Without this grip, a user is unable to select the menu strip at all; it is fixed in the top panel.

TO ADD A DOTTED GRIP TO THE MENU STRIP

1. In the Document Outline window, select the menu strip called *msBrowser*, go to the Properties window, and set the *GripStyle* property to *Visible*.

2. Run the application by pressing F5. Move the menu strip from one panel to the other. You now have an application as cool as Outlook.

Adding a Status Bar to Your Browser

Your application is becoming rich in features, but to get it closer to most Windows applications, you need a status bar to report information about what's going on at any moment during the execution. To accomplish this in your browser, you'll add a StatusStrip control, and within this status strip, you'll add a progress bar.

TO ADD A STATUSSTRIP CONTROL AND A PROGRESS BAR

1. On the form Browser.vb, click the bottom panel handle to expand it. (Note that the glyph arrow direction reverses when you click it.) The tool strip container's bottom panel appears as a blue strip.

2. Drag a StatusStrip control to the tool strip container's bottom panel. After you drop it onto the bottom panel, it should expand to cover the whole panel surface.

MORE INFO

If your application design demands it and if you want to constrain the user in any way, you can also hide panels and prevent users from docking any tool strip or menu strip in a panel. Let's use the current application as an example. If you want to do this, select the tool strip container control named *mainFormTool-StripContainer*. You can select it from either the Properties window or the Document Outline window. Then modify the visible property of the panel you want to hide. For instance, if you would like to hide the bottom panel, set the *BottomToolStripPanelVisible* property to *false*.

3. Rename the StatusStrip control from *StatusStrip1* to *sscBrowser*.

4. Change the *RenderMode* property of the StatusStrip control to *Professional*. This will allow the application to present a status bar to the user using the operating system colors. For instance, if the themes in Windows XP are blue, then the status bar will be blue as well.

5. Add a label control to the status strip by clicking the down arrow of the Status Strip Add control button and then selecting StatusLabel.

6. Rename the control from *ToolStripStatusLabel1* to *lblApplicationStatus*.

7. Add a progress bar to your status strip just as you did for the label control.

8. Rename the control from *ToolStripProgressBar1* to *pbStatus*.

When the status strip and the progress bar are displayed to the user, they usually bring important information about the events that are occurring during execution. Think of it like a letter arriving at your house. You hear the mail truck and realize the mail has arrived. This is the event that is raised. You open your mailbox and the envelope to learn that it's your credit card bill. The bill is one of the pieces of information that comes along with the event. To analogously populate the controls in the status strip, you'll have to configure your application to extract this information from all controls (that is, the envelope) when events are happening (that is, the mail truck arriving). And you'll do that programmatically by writing code in event handlers.

TO POPULATE CONTROLS WITH INFORMATION

1. On the design surface, select the My Own Browser form by clicking its title bar. Look in the Properties window to make sure the Browser form is selected, and click the Events button (yellow lightning) in the Properties window. Find the *Load* event, and double-click it to open the default event handler: *Browser_Load*. (The form *Load* event is raised just before the form is displayed to the user, so, it's a good place to change properties that affect the visual aspects of a form.)

2. Add the following code to the event (*Browser_Load*) to modify the status message label (*lblApplicationStatus*) in the status strip:

```
Me.lblApplicationStatus.Text = "Ready"
```

You'll now attach some code to the progress bar and modify the label on the status strip to indicate to where the user is navigating. When the page is fully downloaded to the client PC, you'll reset the label content in the status strip to the word *Ready*. You'll also modify the browser title to include the URL to where the user navigated. Whenever the OK button is clicked in the Navigate form, the WebBrowser control named *myBrowser* raises the *Navigating* event. That's where you'll start writing code.

3. Select the *myBrowser* control, and then go to the Events list in the Properties window. Double-click the *Navigating* event, and enter the following code:

```
' Modifying the label in the status strip with the URL entered by the user
Me.lblApplicationStatus.Text = "Waiting for: " + e.Url.Host.ToString()
```

Once the user enters a URL and the document is being downloaded, the progress bar will need to update. Periodically, the WebBrowser control raises the *ProgressChanged* event. That's where you'll update the progress bar in the status strip.

4. Make sure you have the *myBrowser* control selected in the Properties window, and then go to the Event list. Double-click the *ProgressChanged* event. Enter the following code (look at the comments to understand the source code):

```
' The CurrentProgress variable from the raised event
' gives you the current number of bytes already downloaded
' while the MaximumProgress is the total number of bytes
' to be downloaded
If e.CurrentProgress < e.MaximumProgress Then
    ' Check if the current progress in the progress bar
    ' is >= to the maximum if yes reset it with the min
    If pbStatus.Value >= pbStatus.Maximum Then
        pbStatus.Value = pbStatus.Minimum
    Else
        ' Just increase the progress bar
        pbStatus.PerformStep()
    End If
Else
    ' When the document is fully downloaded
    ' reset the progress bar to the min (0)
    pbStatus.Value = pbStatus.Minimum
End If
```

When the user's document is fully downloaded, the browser will raise the *DocumentCompleted* event. When this event is raised, the application title needs to be updated to the current URL, and the application status label in the status strip will need to change to the Ready state.

5. In the *myBrowser* event list, double-click the *DocumentCompleted* event. Then add the following code to it:

```
' The validation below is necessary because of asynchronous calls the
' browser is making. We need to make sure it's really done rendering
' the page.
If ((Not (myBrowser.IsBusy)) And (myBrowser.ReadyState = _
   WebBrowserReadyState.Complete)) Then
    'Get Application title using the My namespace
    If My.Application.Info.Title <> "" Then
       Me.Text = My.Application.Info.Title + " - " + e.Url.Host.ToString()
    Else
       'If the application title is missing,
       'use the application name, without the extension
       Me.Text = System.IO.Path.GetFileNameWithoutExtension( _
       My.Application.Info.AssemblyName) + " - " + e.Url.Host.ToString()
    End If
    Me.lblApplicationStatus.Text = "Ready"
End If
```

As you can see, this source code is similar to what you used for the About dialog box and the splash screen. It uses the *My* namespace classes and methods.

6. Save all the files, and run the application now. You should have a working progress bar, and all the new information should be displayed, meaning the modified title window and status strip label.

Personalizing Your Application with Windows Icons

In this section, you'll continue to personalize your browser by adding some icons that come from known Microsoft applications. After this section, you'll have a working Internet browser with most navigational features fully implemented—maybe not with all the functionality of Internet Explorer, but you should be proud of yourself. Look at Figure 6-13 to see what you will have accomplished after this section.

Figure 6-13
Your browser after completing this section

As you can see, you'll implement a nice list of features in this section. Here's what you're going to accomplish:

- Link all buttons to browser functionalities

- Manage the Go button and the Enter key on the Address text box in the tool strip

- Change the Browser form icon to the same globe icon you've set for the application icon on the hard disk

TIP

I suggest you rename your buttons immediately when you add them to make sure the event-handling code has the correct name. It is possible to rename the buttons later, but it's more tedious because you have to perform extra steps, which takes more time. It's just easier, cleaner, and faster to do it as soon as you create the controls.

First you'll add two new tool strips and all their buttons. You'll also add the code to handle all those new buttons. Each time you add a button, rename it before writing the event-handling code. You should do this to make sure you have the correct variable names, which is just a matter of consistency and good practice.

TO ADD TOOL STRIPS AND BUTTONS TO YOUR BROWSER

1. Start by adding two new tool strips to the Browser form right below the menu strip. Name the first one *tsIcons* and the other one *tsNavigation*. Use the Document Outline window to make sure they are under the top panel of the tool strip container that is *mainFormToolStripContainer.TopToolStripPanel*.

2. Select the *tsIcons* tool strip. Then, using the Add Tool Strip Item drop-down list, add six buttons, and name them *tsbBack*, *tsbForward*, *tsbStop*, *tsbRefresh*, *tsbHome*, and *tsbSearch*.

3. To modify the image for each button, change the *Image* property of the ToolStripButton control by clicking the ellipsis button (...) to browse on your hard disk for the icon. Or you can right-click the icon in the tool strip and select Set Image. You'll then have the same dialog box to import the image files from your hard disk. The images for these buttons are all located in the Images folder under Chapter6 where you installed your companion content.

4. For the *tsbSearch* button, right-click the button, select Display Style, and set it to ImageAndText.

5. Modify the *Text* property of the *tsbSearch* button to *Search*. Remember to change all your other controls to meaningful names as well.

6. For each button, add the respective functionality. (You'll see how easy it is to add the desired functionality because the WebBrowser control was well designed by providing methods for the most important functionalities.) Double-click one button after the other, and you'll get to the *Click* event for each one. In each *Click* event, add the code shown for the buttons in Table 6-1.

Button Name	Event Code
tsbBack	myBrowser.GoBack()
tsbForward	myBrowser.GoForward()
tsbStop	myBrowser.Stop()
tsbRefresh	myBrowser.Refresh()
tsbHome	myBrowser.GoHome()
tsbSearch	myBrowser.GoSearch()

Table 6-1
Button Code

7. Run the application, and determine whether the buttons are working. Everything should be working except for the navigation buttons.

You'll now modify the behavior of the two navigation buttons in the *tsbIcons* tool strip to make sure they're enabled only when they should be—that is, when there are pages in the browser's history. When you start the application, the buttons should be turned off. The best place to put this code is the *Load* event of the Browser form. It's a good place because the event will happen right before the user actually sees the form. Next, you need to think about where you should put the code that will enable and disable the two navigation buttons. The ideal place for the validation code is where the navigation occurs because you know at that moment the browser will navigate to a new URL.

TO MODIFY THE BEHAVIOR OF NAVIGATION BUTTONS

1. In Browser.vb, modify *Browser_Load* and *myBrowser_Navigating* to look like the following:

```
Private Sub Browser_Load(ByVal sender As System.Object, ByVal e As
    System.EventArgs) Handles MyBase.Load
    ' Disabling both navigation buttons in the Icons tool strip
    Me.tsbBack.Enabled = False
    Me.tsbForward.Enabled = False
    Me.lblApplicationStatus.Text = "Ready"
```

```
End Sub

Private Sub myBrowser_Navigating(ByVal sender As System.Object, ByVal e
As System.Windows.Forms.WebBrowserNavigatingEventArgs) Handles myBrowser.
Navigating
    ' Add the code to enable or disable whenever there are URLs
    ' in the browsing session's history
    If myBrowser.CanGoBack Then
        tsbBack.Enabled = True
    Else
        tsbBack.Enabled = False
    End If

    If myBrowser.CanGoForward Then
        tsbForward.Enabled = True
    Else
        tsbForward.Enabled = False
    End If

    ' Modifying the label in the status strip with the URL entered by the user
    Me.lblApplicationStatus.Text = "Waiting for: " + e.Url.Host.ToString()
End Sub
```

2. Run the application to determine whether the buttons behave correctly now.

Next, you'll add the names and controls to the *tsNavigation* tool strip as you did for the previous tool strip. However, this time instead of just adding some tool strip buttons, you'll add different types of controls.

For instance, you'll modify the browser to navigate to the URL specified in the text box when the user presses Enter. You'll also modify the behavior of clicking the Go button to make sure it does the same thing.

TO ADD NEW CONTROLS TO THE TSNAVIGATION TOOL STRIP

1. Use the Add Tool Strip Item drop-down list on the *tsNavigation* tool strip, and add the following controls to the tool strip: label, text box, and button. Name the controls *tslblAddress*, *tstbUrl*, and *tsbGo*.

2. Use Table 6-2 to set the properties of the controls.

Control Name	Type	Properties	Value
tslblAddress	ToolStripLabel	Text	Address:
tstbUrl	ToolStripTextBox	Size:Width	350
tsbGo	ToolStripButton	Text	Go
tsbGo	ToolStripButton	DisplayStyle	ImageAndText
tsbGo	ToolStripButton	Image	Go.bmp

Table 6-2
Navigation ToolStrip Controls and Properties

The *tsNavigation* tool strip is not a dialog box with an OK button or a Cancel button, so you cannot use the *AcceptButton* or *CancelButton* property. Therefore, you need to capture another event that will be triggered whenever the user presses Enter.

The *KeyUp* event is triggered whenever the user releases a key. For instance, whenever the user types a letter, he presses the key of the desired letter. When he releases the key, the *KeyUp* event is triggered. The code you'll add in the next exercise will determine whether the key the user just released was the Enter key. If it was, a new method called *NavigateToUrl* will accept a string representing the URL as a parameter and navigate to the URL.

You'll use the same method for the Go button. When you develop an application, you never want to duplicate two pieces of code that differ only by a literal. You always want to reuse the source code whenever possible. The way to do that is to create methods that are generic enough to be used by more than one component. Since the *NavigateToUrl* method has only one line of code, you might be tempted to say that if it's almost the same one line of code, why use a method? The answer is simply that in the future you might have to add some validation. If that one line of code is repeated throughout the source code, you'll have to update it in multiple places. However, if there is only one place where you have to modify the code, your solution is less prone to errors and a lot less tedious.

NOTE

By the way, more than one event is being triggered by pressing the Enter key, but the one that you'll trap is the *KeyUp* event.

TO CONFIGURE THE BROWSER TO NAVIGATE TO THE URL

1. Select the *tstbUrl* tool strip text box.

2. In the event list in the Properties window for *tstbUrl*, double-click the *KeyUp* event. The following is the code to determine whether the user pressed and released the Enter key and also the method *NavigateToUrl* that will enable you to use the same code in more than one place. Add this code to *tstbUrl_KeyUp* and add the *NavigateToUrl* method.

```
Private Sub tstbUrl_KeyUp(ByVal sender As System.Object, ByVal e As System.
Windows.Forms.KeyEventArgs) Handles tstbUrl.KeyUp
    ' e is of type KeyEventArgs and contains all the
    ' information that triggered the event. The KeyCode
    ' is one those information.
    If e.KeyCode = Keys.Enter Then
        Me.NavigateToUrl(tstbUrl.Text)
    End If
End Sub
Private Sub NavigateToUrl(ByVal Url As String)
    Me.myBrowser.Navigate(Url)
End Sub
```

3. Double-click the Go button on the *tsNavigation* tool strip, and add the following code to the *tsbGo_Click* event procedure. (Notice that this is the *NavigateToUrl* method.)

```
Private Sub tsbGo_Click(ByVal sender As System.Object, ByVal e As System.
EventArgs) Handles tsbGo.Click
    Me.NavigateToUrl(tstbUrl.Text)
End Sub
```

You can now modify another piece of code, the Navigate menu *Click* event. You simply have to modify the code so that it calls the *NavigateToUrl* method, as shown here:

```
Private Sub NavigateToolStripMenuItem_Click(ByVal sender As System.Object, ByVal
e As System.EventArgs) Handles NavigateToolStripMenuItem.Click
    If (NavigateWindow.ShowDialog() = Windows.Forms.DialogResult.OK) Then
        Me.NavigateToUrl(NavigateWindow.txtUrl.Text)
    End If
    NavigateWindow.txtUrl.Text = ""
End Sub
```

TO MODIFY THE BROWSER FORM ICON

Finally, you'll modify the Browser form's icon so that the user sees a globe when the browser is running or minimized:

1. Select the Browser form, and then look for the *Icon* property in the Properties window. If you see only events in the Properties window, click the Properties button at the top of the Properties window. Click the ellipsis button (...) to browse for the globe.ico file in the Chapter6 directory in the Images folder under the Chapter6 directory.

The result of your hard labor is the finished product—the My Own Browser application, as shown in Figure 6-14.

Figure 6-14
Finished product—the My Own Browser application

Now that you have enriched your browser application, it is time to refresh it and make it look like a Windows Vista application. To do that, you'll start learning the new Windows Presentation Foundation (WPF). You'll work on the same browser application so that you can focus only on the new topics at hand.

Windows Presentation Foundation

What is WPF? First let's look at where it came from—if you refer to Figure 1-1 in Chapter 1, "Introducing Microsoft Visual Basic 2008 Express Edition," you'll see that WPF was added with the arrival of .NET 3.0 and shipped with Windows Vista. What is it? WPF is a unified programming model that allows developers and designers to build Windows applications that incorporate rich media (sound, video, and so on) and documents.

WPF uses your graphical processing unit (GPU) via a technology called DirectX, which is a software platform and technology that was used mostly for games and other graphical-intensive applications. Programming applications directly with DirectX is not easy, and WPF uses the capabilities of DirectX without the need for you to learn them. With WPF, you have the ability to develop richer applications by using the full power of your computer instead of relying only on your central processing unit (CPU).

With WPF, developers and designers are able to work together to come up with high-quality applications; you probably have seen what WPF will let you do in big Hollywood productions such as *The Net*, *Sneakers*, *Disclosure*, *24*, or *Mission Impossible*. For instance, do you remember in *Disclosure* the virtual glove database with its super innovative explorer software? Or how advanced the e-mail software was? It's always fascinating to see how Hollywood is using software and how good it looks but at the same time how far it is from reality. Well, it's now a reality because of WPF.

Before we dig into the technicalities, I invite you to look at the videos on the Mix07 Web site that showcase WPF capabilities. Specifically, take a look at this nice implementation of a kiosk-based application for a well-known company: *http://sessions.visitmix.com/default.asp?event=1016&session=2017&pid=UNI19&disc=&id=1620&year=2005&search=UNI19*.

NOTE
There are a few differences between WPF on Windows Vista and WPF on earlier versions of Windows. The following two features are unique to Windows Vista: 3D objects get antialiasing only on Windows Vista or newer, and nonrectangular or translucent windows get hardware acceleration (from your graphic card's GPU) only on Windows Vista or newer.

MORE INFO
Many other videos and presentation and learning tools are available from the same Web site. See *http://sessions.visitmix.com/*.

WPF and XAML

Extensible Application Markup Language (XAML), pronounced "zammel," is a use of XML that enables declarative programming in WPF. It is called *declarative programming* because, by using XAML, the developer can define the user interface declaratively, similar to how an XML file describes a document format. It is a programming language because you can create .NET objects by simply using XAML. A good analogy is the new Office 2007 document format that uses XML to describe the structure and formatting of your Word 2007 documents, for instance.

XAML enables something that was really difficult previously: designers and developers working together on the same project. With Visual Studio and Microsoft Expression products such as Microsoft Expression Blend, designers can work on the design and the user interface and then pass them on to the developers so that they can write the code. The video referenced previously is a good example of how these separate activities can come together.

Using XAML simply helps separate the front end, or user interface, from the back end, or business logic. I don't want to get too deep into XAML at this point because that's not the purpose of this book, but we'll start by looking at how XAML defines real .NET objects. Here's how a button is declared in XAML:

```
<Button xmlns="http://schemas.microsoft.com/winfx/2006/xaml/presentation"
Name="btnGo">Go</Button>
```

If you place this code in a file called foo.xaml and then fire up Internet Explorer and open the file, you'll see a big button that takes the entire surface, but it's a real WPF button. You don't need to compile the code, and it works. Isn't that great? This means you can write applications that define your interface and then add events such as the *Click* event and have the code in a separate Visual Basic file; however, it also means it can't run by itself in a browser. It would look like something this:

```
<Button xmlns="http://schemas.microsoft.com/winfx/2006/xaml/presentation"
Name="btnGo" Click="btnGo_click">Go</Button>
```

So, you now see clearly the separation between the user interface definition and the business logic of your application.

WARNING

The goal here is to show how you would create an application in WPF, but Windows Forms is still easier to use and the way to go—unless you are willing to spend some time learning WPF concepts, learning XAML, and working more with the code.

TO CREATE A WPF VERSION OF THE BROWSER

This is an introduction to WPF, so we won't reimplement the whole application here; instead I'll show parts of the Web browser application but with a reduced set of features. In fact, we will implement almost the same version as in Chapter 4.

You'll first define the interface, and then you'll hook up the browser events so that it actually works:

1. Add a new project to your solution by clicking File, Add, New Project. Select the WPF Application template from the Visual Studio templates, and name it MyOwnWpfBrowser. Your screen should look like the one in Figure 6-15. Then click OK to create the project.

   You should now have the new designer surface and XAML editor in a split view on your screen. Look at Figure 6-16 for the new WPF design experience. You'll also notice that the Properties window has changed quite a bit.

Figure 6-15
Adding the WPF browser project to your solution

Microsoft Visual Basic 2008 Express Edition: Build a Program Now!

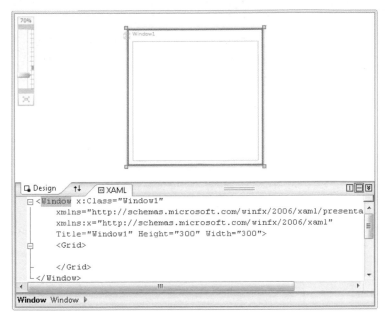

MORE INFO
You can see that this view is rather different. The view is split between Design view at the top and Code view at the bottom. In the bottom part you see the XAML representation of what you see on the design surface. It's a real-time representation, so if you modify either view, you'll see the change immediately replicated in the other. Figure 6-16 shows the horizontal view, but if you click the vertical glyph on the top-right corner of the XAML window, you'll see the screen split in vertical halves instead of horizontal ones. It's a matter of preference which one you use.

Figure 6-16
The new WPF split view design surface and XAML editor

2. Next you'll change the title of this new browser window and change the *Window* variable name. To do this you'll change the XAML directly. Go to the XAML editor, and change the *Title* attribute of the *Window* element to *My Own WPF Browser*. As you do this, look in Design view to see your change being applied in real time. Then change the *Window* variable name by changing the *Class* attribute to *Browser*. The XAML should look like the following at this point:

```
<Window x:Class="Browser"
    xmlns="http://schemas.microsoft.com/winfx/2006/xaml/presentation"
    xmlns:x="http://schemas.microsoft.com/winfx/2006/xaml"
    Title="My Own WPF Browser" Height="300" Width="300">
    <Grid>

    </Grid>
</Window>
```

NOTE

The fact that all of those changes are in sync everywhere makes it easier to learn XAML and WPF because you can see the changes live. Selecting something on the design surface will bring the XAML editor to the corresponding code. So, learning by opening completed samples from the Web helps you learn how to reproduce cool things you see in samples.

3. In Solution Explorer, rename the file Window1.xaml to Browser.xaml, and in the Browser.xaml.vb file change the name of the class to *Browser*.

4. Click the designer surface on the title, and make sure you have the *Window* element selected in the Properties window. Now delete the values for *Height* and *Width* properties, and change *MinHeight* and *MinWeight* to a 640-by-480 window (width by height). You'll see that Design view will resize in real time and that the XAML code changes in real time as well.

If you remember, I was telling you that WPF uses DirectX and the power of your graphic card. Well, a good way to see that is to use the slider on the design surface to adjust the scale and view a really big close-up or zoom out to see the entire window (even if it's bigger than your monitor). This is a really neat feature that displays the great capabilities

of WPF. Look at Figure 6-17, for example: On the left side is WPF, and on the right side is the normal Windows form's title bar but magnified. On the left side you can see how great the title bar characters look and how they don't have a jagged contour. This is possible because WPF uses DirectX and because everything is actually drawn to your design surface.

Figure 6-17
WPF (left) vs. Windows form (right)

5. Save all the files by pressing Ctrl+Shift+S.

6. Now you'll copy the globe icon file you used in the Windows Forms project. In Solution Explorer, right-click the globe.ico file in your Windows Forms browser project, and select Copy. Then right-click your MyOwnWpfBrowser project name in Solution Explorer, and select Paste.

7. You will now set some more *Window* properties. To do this, press Enter just before the **>** in the *Window* element, and add the following XAML:

```
Icon="globe.ico" SizeToContent="WidthAndHeight"
WindowStartupLocation="CenterScreen"
```

8. You have two projects in your solution, so in order to have your WPF browser execute when you press F5, you need to make a small modification to your project. In Solution

Explorer, right-click the MyOwnWpfBrowser project name, and select Set as StartUp Project. Your project name should now be in bold to indicate it will be the one to start when you press F5.

9. This is version 1 of the WPF editor, and some integration and synchronization between Design view/ Code view and Solution Explorer are not without bugs. Before you run the project, you need to modify the project settings. Right-click the project name (MyOwnWpfBrowser), and select Properties. In the Properties window, you should see the Application tab. Locate the Startup URI drop-down list, and select Browser.xaml. Save all the files (by pressing Ctrl+Shift+S).

10. Press F5, and you should get an empty Windows application "WPF style." Look at Figure 6-18 to see what you should see.

You'll now add the two menu items on top of your window: the Navigate and Help menus. For the purpose of this example, we will wire only the Navigate menu. To wire the Navigate menu to an event handler, you will add the *Click* event and then the name of the method to call when clicked. If you look in the following XAML code, you might ask what the *DockPanel* element is; well, it enables you to have easy docking within an element, in this case the *Grid* element.

Figure 6-18
First view of your WPF browser application

1. Select the Browser.xaml file tab at the top of the editor, and then add the following XAML code. Replace all the XAML including the opening and closing *Grid* element. When you're done typing the code, save all the files.

```
<Grid Name="grid1">
    <DockPanel x:Uid="DockPanel_1">
        <! Menu Bar>
        <Menu x:Uid="Menu_1" Background="White" Name="_MainMenu" DockPanel.
        Dock="Top">
```

```
            <! Navigate Menu>
            <MenuItem x:Uid="NavigateMenu" Header="_Navigate" />

            <! Help Menu>
            <MenuItem x:Uid="HelpMenu" Header="_Help">
                <MenuItem x:Uid="AboutMenu" Header="_About" />
            </MenuItem>
        </Menu>
    </DockPanel>
</Grid>
```

2. Next build your solution by hitting Ctrl+Shift+B. To see what it looks like, execute your application by pressing F5. You should see your two menus added to the top of the window.

3. Before we can navigate to the Navigate dialog box when we select the Navigate menu, we need to add this window to our project. To add this new window, right-click the project name, MyOwnWpfBrowser, and select Add and then Window. You'll get the Add New Item dialog box with the Window (WPF) template selected. Change Window1.xaml to Navigate.xaml.

4. In the Navigate.xaml file, delete the current content, and type the following XAML. I'll explain what it means afterward.

```
<Window
    xmlns="http://schemas.microsoft.com/winfx/2006/xaml/presentation"
    xmlns:x="http://schemas.microsoft.com/winfx/2006/xaml"
    x:Class="Navigate"
    Title="Navigate"
    Height="130"
    Width="500"
    ResizeMode="NoResize"
    ShowInTaskbar="False"
    WindowStartupLocation="CenterOwner"
    FocusManager.FocusedElement="{Binding ElementName=Url}">

    <Grid>
        <Grid.Resources>
            <Style TargetType="{x:Type Grid}">
                <Setter Property="Margin" Value="10" />
            </Style>
            <Style TargetType="{x:Type Label}">
                <Setter Property="Margin" Value="30,0,5,5" />
```

```xml
                    <Setter Property="Padding" Value="0,0,0,5" />
                </Style>
                <Style TargetType="{x:Type TextBox}">
                    <Setter Property="Margin" Value="30,0,10,10" />
                    <Setter Property="AutoWordSelection" Value="True" />
                </Style>
                <Style TargetType="{x:Type StackPanel}">
                    <Setter Property="Orientation" Value="Horizontal" />
                    <Setter Property="HorizontalAlignment" Value="Right" />
                </Style>
                <Style TargetType="{x:Type Button}">
                    <Setter Property="Width" Value="70" />
                    <Setter Property="Height" Value="25" />
                    <Setter Property="Margin" Value="5,0,0,0" />
                </Style>
            </Grid.Resources>

        <Grid.ColumnDefinitions>
            <ColumnDefinition Width="Auto" />
            <ColumnDefinition />
        </Grid.ColumnDefinitions>

        <Grid.RowDefinitions>
            <RowDefinition Height="Auto" />
            <RowDefinition Height="Auto" />
            <RowDefinition Height="Auto" />
        </Grid.RowDefinitions>

        <! Label and URL  >
        <Label Grid.Column="0" Grid.ColumnSpan="2" Grid.Row="0">Type an
            Internet address and My Own WPF Browser will open it for you
            </Label>
        <TextBox Name="Url" Grid.ColumnSpan="2" Grid.Column="1" Grid.Row="1">
        </TextBox>

        <! Accept or Cancel >
        <StackPanel Grid.Column="0" Grid.ColumnSpan="2" Grid.Row="2">
            <Button Name="okButton" Click="okButton_Click"
                IsDefault="True">OK</Button>
            <Button Name="cancelButton" IsCancel="True">Cancel</Button>
        </StackPanel>

    </Grid >
</Window>
```

IMPORTANT

You should see a yellow bar at the top of Design view as you're typing indicating that the document root element has been modified. If you want to see the modification, you need to click there to reload the designer. If you do this as you type, you might not be able to see the end result immediately.

You now have a Navigate window in your WPF Designer that should look like the one in Figure 6-19.

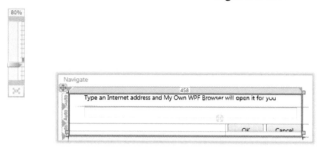

Figure 6-19
Navigate dialog box in the WPF Designer

Now let's return to the XAML code. Most of it is self-explanatory because of the nature of XAML. But one feature was new in this part of the sample: the *Grid.Resources* element in which you've added styles for all elements found in the grid. This has the advantage of not having to set the styles for each individual control. Pretend you had 10 text boxes in your grid; it would be tedious to set the styles for each text box. Well, because of the style definition of *Grid.Resources*, you have to set the styles just once. What follows in the XAML code is the grid layout in terms of columns and rows, and then finally the content of those columns and rows. That's pretty simple, isn't it? You define your user interface, you actually build it piece by piece, and then you attach the functionality in Visual Basic. It's a clear separation of UI and logic!

5. Now, we can't navigate to this dialog box because we didn't wire the *Click* event on the Navigate menu item. To do this, add a click XAML attribute to the Navigate menu item in the Browser.xaml file so that it looks like this:

```
<MenuItem x:Uid="NavigateMenu" Header="_Navigate" click="Navigate_Click" />
```

6. In Solution Explorer, right-click the Browser.xaml file, and select View Code. Replace the content of that file by typing the following VB code:

```
Imports System.Windows.Forms

Public Class Browser
    Inherits Window

    Public Sub New()
        InitializeComponent()
    End Sub

    Private Sub Navigate_Click(ByVal sender As System.Object, ByVal e As
        System.Windows.RoutedEventArgs)
        ' Instantiate the dialog box
        Dim dlg As New Navigate
```

```
                ' Configure the dialog box
                dlg.Owner = Me

                ' Open the dialog box modally
                dlg.ShowDialog()

                ' Process data entered by user if dialog box is accepted
                If (dlg.DialogResult.GetValueOrDefault = True) Then
                    NavigateToUrl(dlg.Url.Text)
                End If

                dlg.Url.Text = ""

        End Sub

        Private Sub NavigateToUrl(ByVal Url As String)

                Dim host As New System.Windows.Forms.Integration.WindowsFormsHost()
                Dim browserControl As New System.Windows.Forms.WebBrowser()

                host.Child = browserControl
                Me.grid1.Children.Add(host)
                browserControl.ScrollBarsEnabled = True
                browserControl.Navigate(Url)
        End Sub
End Class
```

You'll see that the compiler is reporting a few errors. Those errors are there because of a code construct in that file that indicates they are Windows Forms elements. Another possibility is that they are not defined. So, we need to add the references in our project to remove the Windows Forms errors. Not all controls were developed for version 1 of WPF, and you might also have done some investment in Windows Forms that you want to reuse as-is. For that, the .NET Windows client team has developed a class to integrate Windows Forms elements: *WindowsFormsHost*. As you can see in the previous code, we have wrapped the WebBrowser control in an instance of the *WindowsFormsHost* class. By doing this, we enabled the control to execute in a WPF application as if it were a real WPF control. In fact, that is the role of this class. Then by adding the *browserControl* element to the *Grid* element as a child, the WebBrowser control becomes embedded in the grid as any regular WPF control.

MORE INFO

For more information, read the following article on MSDN: *http://msdn2.microsoft.com/ en-us/library/ms751761.aspx*.

7. To remove the errors, let's add *WindowsFormsHost* and *System.Windows.Forms* from the .NET tab in the references for our project. Right-click the MyOwnWpfBrowser project name, and then select Add Reference. Add both references. You'll have to do the operation twice. Once you're done, save all the files, and build your solution.

8. You should have only one error left. The *okButtonClick* event handler is not implemented yet. Select the Navigate.xaml.vb tab, delete all lines in that file, and type the following Visual Basic code:

```
Public Class Navigate
    Inherits Window
    Public Sub New()
        Me.InitializeComponent()
    End Sub

    Private Sub cancelButton_Click(ByVal sender As Object, ByVal e As
        RoutedEventArgs)
        ' Dialog box canceled
        Me.DialogResult = False
    End Sub

    Private Sub okButton_Click(ByVal sender As Object, ByVal e As
        RoutedEventArgs)
        MyBase.DialogResult = New Nullable(Of Boolean)(True)
    End Sub
End Class
```

NOTE

The sample WPF browser you just created was done this way for learning purposes. If you do real development in WPF, there are a set of best practices to follow that would enable you to have your application translated for different languages. Other design principles apply to the best practices, so if you go on to develop applications commercially in WPF, please read MSDN for all those best practices.

9. Save all the files, build your solution, and then execute your application.

You should have a functional Web browser developed in WPF. We won't implement more of the Web browser in WPF in this chapter because the goal was to show how different the development approaches are and how a bit more tedious it is for beginner developers to develop in WPF. Nevertheless, I am not discouraging you to use WPF—quite the opposite. I invite you to develop your first applications like we did in this book. When you develop an application for learning purposes, develop both at the same time, one in Windows Form and one in WPF. That way you'll become more proficient in WPF, and you can then go to more advanced topics.

In Summary...

In this chapter, you took a simple application and upgraded it to create a professional-looking application with many nice features for your users. You learned to add a splash screen to your application and to work with dialog boxes. You created an About dialog box and a Navigate dialog box to allow your users to navigate to a URL, and you added an autocomplete feature to your text boxes and the autosuggest/append feature by using the browser's URL history. You then added tool strips, progress bars, and icons from Windows. You dynamically managed controls, and you learned a lot about new events and how to handle them using event arguments.

After finishing the Windows Forms implementation, you learned how to add a second project and created a WPF Web browser. While doing this, you experimented with XAML and the WPF development technique. You implemented a dialog box that allowed you to enter a URL and navigate to it. You then learned how to use a Windows Forms control in WPF to create a hybrid application.

In the next chapter, you'll learn techniques to use when things don't go well; that is, you'll learn the art of debugging code. You'll also learn about the Edit and Continue feature, the new data visualizers, tips and tricks, and much more.

Chapter 7

Fixing the Broken Blocks

As you'll discover more and more, when you develop an application, you rarely succeed on your first attempt. Most of the time, the process goes like this: brainstorm on paper, look at the users' needs (often yours), perform some analysis, prototype, design, develop, test, fix bugs, test the product again, and finally release it. This is a high-level view of the process; it can be much more complicated or simplified. It all depends on the complexity of the project, the number of people involved, and so on. But this is certain: you always need to debug your applications, and Microsoft Visual Basic 2008 provides many tools to help you fix your bugs faster.

To show you how to use the tools and techniques to debug your applications, I've created a sample application that you'll use in this chapter. If you installed the companion content at the default location, the application should be at the following location on your hard disk: Documents\Microsoft Press\VB 2008 Express\Chapter7\. Look for a folder named Debugger Start in the Chapter7 folder. Double-click the Debugger.sln solution.

This solution has several items you have not learned about yet. First, the solution has more than one project. This is a common practice in developing applications. In this case, the solution (named Debugger) contains two projects: a Windows Forms application named Debugger and a managed library named MyLibrary (a managed DLL). The acronym DLL stands for Dynamic Link Library; a DLL is a library of classes and their methods that are called dynamically and as needed by an application. A DLL doesn't contain a main entry point and cannot be executed by itself. Also, multiple applications can use the same DLL at the same time.

Second, the project Debugger has a type of file you haven't seen yet: a text file. You can have different kinds of files in your projects, and a text file is not uncommon. In this case, one of the methods called by the Debugger.exe application will use the text file, so to have the file in the output folder, you need to select it in Solution Explorer and then change the *Copy to Output Directory* property to *Copy If Newer*.

Using a DLL in an Application

When you design an application, you usually have more than one component. In many cases, the components are new classes (types). It is good practice to have those types in a separate source code file instead of keeping them with the user interface code. Often, the classes are grouped in a single library or DLL.

When you want to use a type from a library, you need to make your application aware of all the types and methods contained in that library by adding a reference to the library in the application.

> **NOTE**
>
> The Debugger program is exclusively for the educational purposes of this chapter. It doesn't do anything interesting except teach debugging.

126

Microsoft Visual Basic 2008 Express Edition: Build a Program Now!

TO ADD A REFERENCE TO YOUR APPLICATION

1. Select the project where you want to add the reference; in this case, select Debugger.

2. Right-click Debugger (look at Figure 7-1 to make sure you're at the right place), and then select Add Reference.

   As you can see from the tabs on the dialog box that appears, references can come from multiple sources.

3. Select the Projects tab, and then select the MyLibrary project, which contains the managed DLL. Click OK to add the reference to your project.

Because the DLL is in the same solution and you just added a reference to that DLL to your application, Microsoft Visual Studio now knows there is a dependency between the two and will always build the DLL first so that your application builds the binary with the most up-to-date DLL possible.

You can verify that the reference has been inserted in two ways:

- Open the Project Designer (by right-clicking the project name in Solution Explorer and choosing Properties), and select the References tab on the left side, as shown in Figure 7-2.

- Click the Show All Files button in Solution Explorer, and expand References.

Figure 7-1
Add Reference menu choice from the Debugger project

Reference Name	Type	Vers...	Copy Local	Path
MyLibrary	.NET	0.0.0.0	True	C:\Users\
System	.NET	2.0.0.0	False	C:\Windov
System.Data	.NET	2.0.0.0	False	C:\Windov
System.Deployment	.NET	2.0.0.0	False	C:\Windov
System.Drawing	.NET	2.0.0.0	False	C:\Windov
System.Windows.Forms	.NET	2.0.0.0	False	C:\Windov
System.Xml	.NET	2.0.0.0	False	C:\Windov

Figure 7-2
Project Designer's References tab showing the MyLibrary reference

Using one of these methods, you'll see the reference to MyLibrary. When you're done adding the reference, your application can create instances of the new types that are built in the DLL and use them appropriately. The build process (compiler and linker) will now accept the use of those new types; however, for Visual Studio to have those new types available via IntelliSense and for the compiler to know about those new types, one more step is required. You might already have seen the first line of code in the TestApplication.vb file. The line reads *Imports MyLibrary*.

What the *Imports* statement essentially does is import namespaces or programming elements, such as new types, that are defined in referenced projects and assemblies. By adding this line of code, you're telling Visual Studio to look into that assembly for the metadata that will enable IntelliSense to be populated with the public/protected elements and be used at build time by the compiler. After adding this line, you'll gain access to those items whenever you have an instance of one of the types built in the library.

Using Breakpoints, Locals, Edit and Continue, and Visualizers

TIP
If the breakpoints don't appear, you can add them by clicking in the left margin.

There is no better way to dive into this subject than by going through the code. If the TestApplication.vb source code file is not already open, open it by right-clicking the TestApplication.vb file and selecting View Code. You should see red dots on the left side of the screen; those red dots are breakpoints. Figure 7-3 shows the source code and the breakpoints.

```
Imports MyLibrary
Imports System.IO

Public Class TestApplication

    Private Sub btn_Click(ByVal sender As System.Object, ByVal e As Syste
        Dim myObjectLibrary As New Library()
        Dim myString As String = "Helloworld"

        MessageBox.Show(myObjectLibrary.Divide(5, 3).ToString())
        MessageBox.Show(myObjectLibrary.Divide(3, 3).ToString())
        MessageBox.Show(myObjectLibrary.ReadFile("MyExistingTextFile.txt"
        myObjectLibrary.ManipulateStrings(myString, 20)
        MessageBox.Show(myString)
        myObjectLibrary.ManipulateStrings(myString, 1)
        MessageBox.Show(myString)
        MessageBox.Show(myObjectLibrary.Divide(6, 4).ToString())
        MessageBox.Show(myObjectLibrary.ReadFile("MyNotExistingTextFile.t
```

Figure 7-3
Source code and breakpoints from the TestApplication Windows form

When the debugger encounters a breakpoint, it stops executing the application. In this source code, one breakpoint is placed on the call to *MessageBox.Show(myString)*. Another breakpoint appears in Library.vb in the first line of code of the *Divide* method. In the following procedure, you will execute the code and go through a debugging session.

To debug an application, you can do one of the following:

- Press F5, or click the Start Debugging button. The program will start executing normally. If there is a breakpoint in the source code, the execution will stop there. Otherwise, the program will continue to execute unless there is an unhandled exception or error.

- Alternatively, you can debug the application by stepping through the code line by line. To do this, press F8, or click the Step Into button.

For now, you'll jump to the first breakpoint and execute the code in the sample program using the first technique.

TO BEGIN DEBUGGING AN APPLICATION

1. Press F5, or click the Start Debugging button.

2. You will see a Try Me! button. Click it. The code should stop executing at the first breakpoint in the *Divide* method, and you should see what is shown in Figure 7-4. The yellow highlighted line indicates the next statement to be executed.

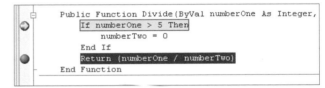

Figure 7-4
Execution stopped at the first breakpoint in the Divide *method*

You're now in debugging mode, so you have access to a plethora of tools and data elements about your application to help you understand what is happening when your application is executed. You can see the content of local variables, parameters, exception messages, the console window, and many more items you'll discover in the next few pages. All of that information is useful when an application is not behaving the way it should and you're trying to understand why. With all the information the debugger provides, you can try to uncover where the problem lies and see why you have a bug. You can also use the debugger for learning purposes as you are doing right now. The debugger is an excellent teacher when you're new to a technology, when you're new to a language construct, or when you're simply trying to understand a certain element. It is also common to use the debugger to understand someone else's code, and it is especially helpful when you need to modify existing code.

You'll now look at the first series of data elements offered by the debugger while you're stepping through your code. At the bottom of the Visual Studio screen, you can see a series of tabs, which can include Locals, Watch, Immediate Window, Output, and Error List. If you don't see these tabs, you can open these tabs by selecting them in the View and Debug menus. Most of these are not visible when you are working in editing mode. You saw in Chapter 3, "Creating Your First Applications," that the Error List is there only to show the results of the real-time compilation. While you're debugging, the Locals tab is usually on top and shows the current variables and object information. If the Locals tab is not displayed, you can add it and the Watch tab by selecting Windows on the Debug menu. Look at Figure 7-5 to see the tabs from your debugging session.

Figure 7-5
Tabs present during debugging in Visual Studio

On the Locals tab, you can see four elements of data from your *Divide* method: *Me*, *Divide*, *numberOne*, and *numberTwo*. These are, in order, the instance of the current object, the return value for the function named *Divide*, and the two parameters. The debugger detects all elements that are in scope in that method and displays them on the Locals tab. The elements in scope are all the elements that are "visible" from where the instruction pointer (that is, the next instruction to be executed) is located. In this case, it could be either local variables or shared variables. This means that throughout the execution of the *Divide* method, you'll be able to follow the values that those items will have. Now it's your turn to see this for yourself.

TO CONTINUE DEBUGGING THE APPLICATION

1. Press F8, or click the Step Into button. Then press F8 to get to the division operation.

   While debugging, you can always hover the mouse pointer over program elements to get the information you would otherwise find on the Locals tab. For instance, if you hover your mouse pointer over the *numberOne* element, you'll see the same value that is shown on the Locals tab, as illustrated in Figure 7-6.

2. Execute the next line of code by pressing F8 or clicking the Step Into button.

I'll now explain what is going on from the compiler's perspective. On the Locals tab, the *Divide* element (the return value of that function) contains the result of 5 divided by 3, which should be 1.

But why does the debugger show 2? You just found a bug. (Note: I've inserted this error to demonstrate how small mistakes can create bigger problems.) If you hover the mouse pointer over the / operator, you'll see the word *double*. Press F1, and search for the / operator in Help. You'll find that the result produced by this operator depends on the types of the two operands used in the operation. In this case, the / operator uses two integers. When you use the / operator with two integers, the result is a double. The result is the full quotient plus the remainder, or 2.

Figure 7-6
Getting the value of the numberOne *local variable in two different ways*

At the same location in the Help system, you'll see that the integer division this function was supposed to use is actually the \ operator.

CAUTION

The Edit and Continue feature doesn't work on 64-bit operating systems.

At this point, you would ordinarily click the Stop Debugging button, but a new feature in Visual Basic 2008 allows you to modify your code and verify immediately whether the change you make solves the problem. This feature is called Edit and Continue. As its name implies, the Edit and Continue feature lets you edit an element in the application and continue the execution. In fact, not only can you do this, but you can also modify the next instruction to execute, change the value of a variable, and re-execute the instruction. This can be a huge time-saver because you don't have to stop the execution, make the change, rebuild, and re-execute the new code. You can see the changes right away.

3. Go to the left side, where the yellow arrow indicates the next instruction to be executed. When you hover your mouse pointer over the yellow arrow, you should see a transparent arrow indicating you can move the yellow arrow. Click and hold the yellow arrow, and slide it up and back over the division instruction.

4. Change the / operator to the \ operator, and then re-execute the instruction by pressing F8 or clicking the Step Into button.

NOTE

There are some limitations to the edits you can make with Edit and Continue. To see a complete list of limitations, simply perform a search in the Help system with the following search criteria: *Edit and Continue [Visual Basic]*. Then look for the two sections about unsupported features that explain what you can't do.

5. Look at the Locals tab, and you'll see that the *Divide* element now has the value 1, which is correct. You've just fixed your first real bug; you're a better developer now!

6. Save your file, and then step into the code until you see a message box with 1 for the first division. If you don't see the message box, you might need to switch to it on the Windows taskbar. Click OK in the message box. Continue stepping into the code until you return to the *Divide* method with a new set of values and you're pointing at the first instruction in the method.

When you're back to the *Divide* method, you will not re-execute every instruction because you know that the method should now execute correctly. Instead, you'll step out of the code using the Step Out function. Stepping out doesn't mean you'll skip the execution; stepping out simply means that the debugger will execute all the instructions of the current method and go back to the calling point. If you do it on a single instruction, it will simply execute it.

TO STEP OUT OF THE CODE

1. In the Library.vb file, click the red dot at the first breakpoint of the *Divide* method. Clicking the red dot removes the breakpoint. The red dot should now be gone.

2. In addition to clicking the red dot, you can disable the second breakpoint by using one of three other methods:

   ■ Right-click the line of code that has the breakpoint, click the Breakpoint menu choice, and then click the Delete Breakpoint choice. Look at Figure 7-7 to see this in action.

   ■ Click the Debug menu, and then select Toggle Breakpoint or press F9.

   ■ Right-click the red dot indicating the breakpoint, and select the only available choice: Delete Breakpoint.

Figure 7-7
Deleting a breakpoint by using a contextual menu in the code editor

3. You should be at the first line of code in the *Divide* method. Now that you're in the *Divide* method, you can press Ctrl+Shift+F8 to step out of the *Divide* method, or you can click the Step Out button. This will execute all the instructions in that method and return to the caller.

4. Press F5 to execute all the methods up to the next breakpoint.

   You should see another message box with the result 1. Click OK, and then you should be stopped in the source code of the *ReadFile* method.

5. The *ReadToEnd* method reads the content of the open file and puts it into a string variable. Press Ctrl+Shift+F8 and then F8. A message box should display the string variable content. Click OK in the message box. You should now be back at the caller.

6. Step into the code until you get the string *Helloworld* in a message box. Pay attention to the order of execution, and look into the variables and content in each of the tab sections.

7. Click OK in the message box, and then step into the code again to get into the *ManipulateStrings* method.

The first instruction (apart from the variable declaration) in the *ManipulateStrings* method is taking the string received in the argument and converting it to an array of characters. The reason for converting the string is that strings are immutable in .NET, and therefore you have to work with them in read-only mode once they're created. Methods modifying a string are actually returning a new string object that contains the modification applied to it.

Therefore, if you want to modify a string character by character, or if you want to access one single character in a string by using an index, you first need to convert the string into an array of characters.

TO BEGIN STEPPING OUT OF THE *MANIPULATESTRINGS* METHOD

1. Press Ctrl+Shift+F8 to step out of the *ManipulateStrings* method, or click the Step Out button.

The first invocation of the method is fine. At the second invocation, however, the application stops abruptly. What just happened is an *unhandled* exception. An unhandled exception happens whenever an error occurs that is not anticipated or handled explicitly by your application. In that case, the execution of your application is halted because there is no way

MORE INFO

The *Using* block in the *ReadFile* method guarantees that you're going to dispose of the resources you're using when you exit the block delimited by *End Using*. You can read more about this by doing a search in the Help system by using the *Using* statement as a keyword in the Look For text box.

MORE INFO

As you can see in the source code, one of the *ManipulateStrings* arguments, *myString*, is passed with the *ByRef* keyword. When you have an argument that is passed to a method by reference, the called method is receiving a reference to the same memory location used by the caller. Therefore, if the method is modifying the content of that argument, it is modifying the content at this memory location and thus modifying the variable from the caller. In this case, anything that is done to the *myString* argument will modify the value of the variable in the calling code. The other argument is *myPosition*, and it is passed with the *ByVal* keyword. When you have an argument that is passed by value, the method is receiving a copy of the variable from the calling code and thus can't modify the original value from the caller. Therefore, the content will get lost when the method ends and the execution flow returns to the caller.

the application can continue in that state without potentially corrupting the memory or opening security holes. One of the .NET runtime (CLR) principles is to make sure that neither ever happens. Therefore, the CLR crashes your application to prevent your application from continuing to execute in an unknown state. Even though the CLR is taking those precautions, it is less likely to have insecure code executing in .NET; however, it is still possible.

To help you find the bug that raised the unhandled exception, Visual Studio includes another useful tool: the Exception Assistant. The assistant is helpful because, based on the context of the exception, it provides information that helps you debug, including error helpers such as the type of exception, troubleshooting tips, and corrective actions that may be applied through the Exception Assistant. Look at Figure 7-8 to see the information provided for the current exception.

Figure 7-8
Exception Assistant

When you look at the exception name, the troubleshooting tips, and the data visualizers, it should be apparent why an unhandled exception was raised. The exception name alone is self-explanatory: *IndexOutOfRangeException*. The first troubleshooting tip displayed asks you to make sure the maximum index on a list is less than the list size. Arrays in .NET are *zero-based*, which means that the first element starts at index 0. The length of the string received as the argument is 10, as shown in Figure 7-8.

The intent of this method was to modify the last character of the string when the position in the array is equal to a position passed by value to the method. In this particular case, the position passed by value to the method is 1.

Therefore, in the *For* loop, at the second character of that string, the *If* statement will return *true*, and then the index *i* will get the value of the string *length*. This means *i* is now equal to 10. When the application tries to modify the character at index 10, an exception is generated because index 10 is outside the range of the array. The array has 10 characters, with indexes from 0 to 9. Figure 7-9 uses a new visualizer to look at the *CharArray* content.

Figure 7-9
Array visualizer

When you move the mouse pointer over program elements, you'll sometimes see a magnifier. If you click the drop-down list, you will see a list of visualizers that display the information in a way that is meaningful to the data type you're seeing. For instance, if you're working with XML or HTML content, the XML or HTML visualizer will allow you to see the content as if you were using Windows Internet Explorer or any other XML/HTML tool. You'll use one of the visualizers soon when you debug the *ReadFile* method.

CAUTION
If at any time you use the Edit and Continue feature and you see that your data is odd-looking or seems corrupted, stop the debugging process and restart the debugging of your application.

TO FIX THE OUT-OF-RANGE PROBLEM

1. Modify the *ManipulateStrings* method. Subtract 1 from the string *length* when you assign a new value to *i*. The line of code should look like this after you modify it:

```
i = myString.Length - 1
```

2. After modifying this line of code, move your next execution pointer to the *For* statement so that index *i* starts at 0. Step through the code or step out. This time there should be no exception. Continue to step through the code, and you should now see another message: "HelloworlZ." The string has been modified because it was passed by reference.

Continue to step through the code, and soon you'll get a second exception, which is a division-by-zero error. Of course, an exception is raised because the *Divide* method assigns 0 to the denominator when the numerator is greater than 5. Using a visualizer, you can see that the numerator is 6, and therefore 0 will be assigned to the denominator.

Again, the first displayed troubleshooting tip helps by suggesting that you make sure the denominator is not 0. To solve the problem, you could add an *If* statement; but before you do that, consider another .NET principle.

It's good practice in .NET to use the exception mechanism to catch those corner cases instead of coding special conditional instructions that bloat the code. The exceptions are an integral part of the .NET Framework, and they're everywhere. I'll now explain the logic behind this decision.

In a real application, your application would not purposely assign 0 to the denominator; therefore, most divisions would result in a correct operation. Adding an *If* statement would result in a conditional instruction executed for every single division. And because most divisions would be valid, you would automatically slow down your application. Using an exception-handling mechanism to catch those corner cases is a much better solution because the exception-handling code will be executed only when necessary, so your application should be faster.

When you insert exception-handling code in your application, it is best practice to always catch exceptions from the most precise to the least precise. In this case, you know that the *DivisionByZeroException* exception is the one most likely to occur; therefore, it's the first one you want to catch.

When you catch an exception, the exception is "handled." You then need to do something about it; either you handle it by mentioning it to the user or you throw the exception back. In this case, you want the user to know that an exception was raised, but you don't want the program to crash. Here's an example that demonstrates this form of handling that I'm sure you already know. If you try to divide by zero in Microsoft Office Excel, Excel won't crash; it will simply indicate that your entry results in a division-by-zero error and displays the #DIV/0! message in the cell.

An older way of doing things was to make your method return an integer to indicate success or failure. And that's where people met with trouble because between two applications, and sometimes between two functions, the same integer code meant two different things. You received an integer that was supposed to tell you why your application failed, but the originating code had two meanings, and it was a nightmare to figure out which one was the valid error code. In addition, when people used error codes, their code was ugly because they either had a switch case or had a series of nested *If* statements.

In .NET, you should never design your methods to return an integer to indicate success or failure, and you shouldn't use a Boolean for the same purpose. This is a poor practice that was used when exceptions did not exist or when people didn't know or want to use them appropriately. *You should never do this.* Instead, use exceptions.

TO ADD CODE TO HANDLE DIFFERENT EXCEPTIONS

1. Click the Stop Debugging button, or press Ctrl+Alt+Break to stop debugging mode. In TestApplication.vb, modify the *btn_Click* method to look like the following:

```
Dim myObjectLibrary as New Library()
Dim myString As String = "Helloworld"
Dim myFile As String = ""

Try
   MessageBox.Show(myObjectLibrary.Divide(5, 3).ToString())
   MessageBox.Show(myObjectLibrary.Divide(3, 3).ToString())
   MessageBox.Show(myObjectLibrary.Divide(6, 4).ToString())
Catch ex As DivideByZeroException
   MessageBox.Show(ex.ToString())
End Try

Try
   myFile = "MyExistingTextFile.txt"
   MessageBox.Show(myObjectLibrary.ReadFile(myFile))
   myFile = "MyNotExistingTextFile.txt"
   MessageBox.Show(myObjectLibrary.ReadFile(myFile))
Catch ex As FileNotFoundException
   MessageBox.Show(myFile + " doesn't exist!")
End Try

myObjectLibrary.ManipulateStrings(myString, 20)
MessageBox.Show(myString)
myObjectLibrary.ManipulateStrings(myString, 1)
MessageBox.Show(myString)
```

2. Remove all the breakpoints in TestApplication.vb and Library.vb, and execute the code. Look at the different message boxes. If a *DivideByZeroException* or *FileNotFoundException* exception occurs, a message box will be displayed.

During this debugging session, you didn't use some other useful tabs. For instance, the Watch tab is important because you can enter variables and expressions that you want to follow and monitor during the execution of the application.

Another useful tool is the Immediate window, where you can type anything and the compiler verifies, compiles, and executes it on the fly! Any effect on the application you are debugging is immediate. Any piece of code that can be evaluated by the compiler and does not require a block of code can be entered in the Immediate window. You could enter a loop, for instance. You also have full access to IntelliSense in this window just as if you were in the code editor. Let's look at a simple example.

TO USE THE IMMEDIATE WINDOW

1. Put a breakpoint at the first instruction in your application, and run the application by pressing F5.

2. If you don't see the Immediate window, just click the Debug menu, and then click Windows and Immediate. You should have an empty Immediate window at the bottom of your screen.

3. Type **i = 5**, and then hit the Try-It button.

4. Type **If i > 2 Then MessageBox.Show(i)**, and then press Enter.

The message box that appears should show a 5. You can test code in real time during the execution without executing a single line of code from your application. But beware that if you use variables that are in your application and modify them in the Immediate window, you modify them for the application as well.

5. Click the Stop Debugging button to stop executing the application.

You're now not only able to build new applications, but you're also aware of the techniques and tools available to debug them.

In Summary...

In this chapter, you learned about breakpoints; about different techniques to step into, step over, and step out of the source code; and about data visualizers to see the data in the most pertinent way based on its content or context. You also learned how to work with a DLL.

You discovered that you can use the Edit and Continue feature to modify variables at run time and continue the execution.

You learned how you can move the next instruction pointer to re-execute some lines of code. You also started to deal with exceptions and learned the dos and don'ts of debugging. You saw how subtle bugs can find their way in—usually because of distractions and some-times simply because you don't possess all of the knowledge and experience yet—but that's OK. Don't worry; you're in a process called *learning*.

In the next chapter, you'll learn about using databases, working with ADO.NET, using LINQ, and manipulating data to and from a Microsoft SQL Server Express Edition database. You'll learn how to use this data to populate controls on a Windows form. You'll also learn how to create an application to add, modify, delete, and visualize rows in a car tracker application.

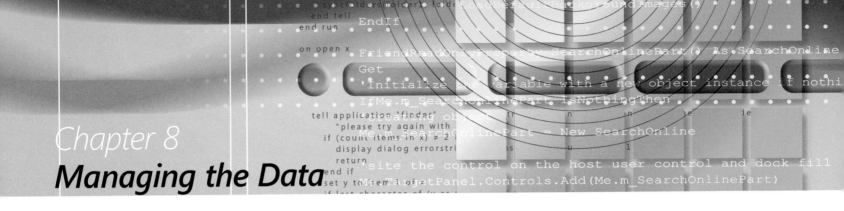

Chapter 8
Managing the Data

So far, you've seen how to build a Windows Forms application and examples of the characteristics that type of application has, but you have not managed a great deal of data. Managing data is always a concern, whether at home, at the office, at school, or even for recreation. For instance, I have many recipes and ideas for great dinners, but when I want to prepare a nice meal, it takes me so much time to find the recipes that usually I change my mind about cooking. If I had this information in my computer, it would be easy to quickly access my recipe for rack of lamb with herb crust and prepare a fabulous meal. I could also add other pertinent information to the recipe file, such as what side dishes were served with the main dish or what wines went well with this recipe. I could even add a picture of the finished meal.

You can manage some data using a word processing program, such as Microsoft Word, but it would become unmanageable as soon as you collect a lot of recipes and need to search for information within that file. Using a spreadsheet program, such as Microsoft Excel, is also problematic. Trying to find information quickly when using more than one variable is close to impossible. Using the recipe example, suppose you want to retrieve all the recipes that can serve at least six people and that have lamb stew meat but no mint in the ingredients because one of your guests is allergic to mint. Imagine the time it would take to find that information in either a Word file or an Excel spreadsheet. That's where databases come to the rescue.

In this chapter, you'll learn what a database is; how to create a database; how to add, delete, and update data; how to search or query a database;

and how to use a database in a Windows Forms application. Accompanying Microsoft Visual Basic 2008 Express Edition is Microsoft SQL Server 2005 Express Edition, which is a fully workable version of its big brother, Microsoft SQL Server 2005, but with fewer features. SQL Server 2005 Express Edition is free, easy to use, and geared toward building simple and dynamic applications.

What Is a Database?

A *database* is a collection of data that is stored in files on disks using a systematic structure. Because of this systematic structure, users can query the data using management software called a *database management system* (DBMS). SQL Server 2005 is a *relational database management system* (RDBMS), which means its data is structured using sets (the sets theory in mathematics) and logical relations (predicates). Most commercial database products are based on the relational model. In fact, it has been one of the most popular models for the past 20 years. Apart from Microsoft SQL Server, you might have also heard of Oracle or IBM DB2.

NOTE

You'll learn about some of the other elements contained in a relational database later in this chapter.

What's in a Database?

A relational database, such as SQL Server 2005, contains multiple tables that are related. A database can also contain views, stored procedures, functions, indexes, security information, and other elements. In this section, you'll learn about the basic elements of a relational database, which are a table and its components.

A *table* contains columns and rows. A *column* defines the type of data, and a *row* contains the actual data. Because the relational model has strict rules, an RDBMS that uses the relation model must implement them.

MORE INFO

In reality, no popular RDBMS is fully implementing the pure relational model as it was first created in the 1970s.

What Are Data Normalization and Data Integrity?

The rules defining the relational model are called *normalization rules*. Normalization is a process that data architects apply whenever they are at the design phase. Normalization rules exist to reduce the chance of having the same data stored in more than one table; in other words, they reduce the level of redundancy and preserve data integrity in the database. Logically, the normalization process exists to help place data into its own table so that no duplication of information occurs in more than one table. For example, having an application in which a customer's address, city, state or province, ZIP or postal code, and country are duplicated in two different tables is a bad idea. There should be only one link from the customer table to the other table referencing additional customer information. Having duplicate data makes updates and deletions more problematic and also poses the risk of having modified data in one table and not the other. This example demonstrates a data integrity problem.

Let's look at another data integrity problem. Suppose you have both a product table and a table containing customer order details. Although you normalized your data, data integrity does not exist in this example. Why? Let's say you decide to delete product1, which means removing the row from the product table that corresponds to product1. If the RDBMS would let you do this, it would mean that suddenly all rows in the customer order details table that contained this product would not be able to show which product was ordered because the product would no longer exist. Those rows would be *orphaned*, which could have disastrous results for the company and the application.

As you can see, data integrity is an important concept related to the accuracy, validity, and correctness of the data. To better understand some of these concepts, let's look at another example.

Suppose you are the owner of an online store and want to manage your company using a software application. To use a software application, you must start thinking about using a database. Any company, both small and large, typically has a great deal of data to store. Also, because data is all around us, people want more access to this data so they can create reports and conduct analysis. That is why databases are so useful. Returning to your online store, at a minimum you would like to store information about your customers, products, invoices, purchasing, and inventory. To summarize all these areas, let's take a look at the Product, OrderHeader, and OrderDetail tables, as shown in Table 8-1, Table 8-2, and Table 8-3, respectively.

> **NOTE**
> The following tables have purposely been kept simple (some columns are missing) to illustrate the concepts you've just learned.

Column Name	Data Type	Allow Nulls?
ProductID (PK)	Integer	Not Null
ProductNumber	nvarchar(10)	Not Null
Name	nvarchar(50)	Not Null
Description	nvarchar(200)	Null
Photo	image	Null
Price	money	Not Null
Taxable	bit	Not Null

Table 8-1
Product Table

Column Name	Data Type	Allow Nulls?
OrderID (PK)	integer	Not Null
OrderDate	datetime	Not Null
DueDate	datetime	Not Null
CustomerID (FK)	integer	Not Null
TaxAmount	money	Not Null
Total	money	Not Null

Table 8-2
OrderHeader Table

Column Name	Data Type	Allow Nulls?
OrderID (PK) (FK)	integer	Not Null
OrderDetailID (PK)	integer	Not Null
ProductID (FK)	integer	Not Null
Quantity	integer	Not Null
LineTotal	numeric(38,6)	Not Null

Table 8-3
OrderDetail Table

You can also represent your Product, OrderHeader, and OrderDetail tables graphically, as shown in Figure 8-1. This is a common way of looking at databases.

Figure 8-1
Partial database diagram for a small online company

What Is Null?

One of your first observations about the tables is that they each have an Allow Nulls? column, which is also reflected in Figure 8-1. When designing a table, you need to consider what's absolutely necessary (Not Null) and what's not (Null). For instance, when you insert a new row into the Product table, it might not matter whether the product has a photo, but it might be a problem to have a product without a product number. Now let's correlate how allowing null is related to data integrity. Whenever a table is designed with columns that don't allow null, the RDBMS will reject any insertion of a new row that has a column set to null when it is not supposed to be. When you pay attention to those columns that cannot be set to null when designing your tables, you automatically add another data integrity layer by making sure that all the necessary data is present before the record is inserted into the database.

What Are Primary Keys and Foreign Keys?

You can see in the previous tables that some columns are marked "(PK)," which stands for *primary key*. In Figure 8-1, primary key columns are marked with a yellow key. Some other columns are identified with "(FK)" to indicate that these columns are *foreign keys*. Let's start by talking about the primary key.

Primary Keys

A *primary key* is a value that is used to uniquely identify a specific row in a table. A primary key has the following attributes:

- Can be composed of one or more column names. When it's composed of more than one column, it's called a *composite key*.

- Is often a numeric field.

- Is often generated by the RDBMS, in which case it's called a *surrogate key*. A surrogate key is frequently (but not always) a sequential number. A surrogate key is also called an *identity* in SQL Server 2005. An identity starts at a set number, called the *identity seed*, and increments by another set number, called the *identity increment*. For example, if you create a table named Product, you can have a column named ProductID that is set as an identity, and you can set the identity seed to 1 with an identity increment to 1. When the first row is created in the Product table, the ProductID will be generated by the RDBMS and set to 1. The following row will have a ProductID that is set to 2, and so forth.

- Should be as small as possible but large enough to support the number of rows it will represent.

- Is immutable, meaning its value should never change.

- Is also a natural key when the key has a logical relationship with the rest of the columns in the table. For example, if you had a book table, the ISBN number could be used as a primary key because it uniquely identifies one book. It would be an advantage compared with a generated key because it would take less space and has to exist anyway!

- Is also used to relate two tables together.

In our Product table example, ProductID is the primary key. At design time, it will also be an identity. You can claim that the product number could be a primary key—and you could be right—but in certain scenarios a product number could be used twice. For example, suppose you have product #FG-001 with a revision 1.0. In time, you change the product because of customer complaints and give it a revision 2.0. You want your customers to continue to order the same product number for many business reasons. In your database, you would retire the product revision 1.0 by perhaps changing a column named Active, and you would then add another row in your table with the new product details including revision 2.0 and set it to Active. Why can't you use the same row? Let's assume that six months after creating the new product revision, you want to create a graph to determine whether your changes to the product mean you had fewer returns from your customers. It would be difficult to come up with good data if you had only one row for the product, but it would be fairly easy to do if you have two rows because they would be unique in the database, with each having a different ProductID.

In the OrderDetail table, you have a composite primary key that is a combination of OrderID and OrderDetailID. This means these two columns would ensure the uniqueness of a row in the OrderDetail table. In the OrderHeader table, OrderID is the primary key.

Foreign Keys

A *foreign key* is a column in a table that relates to a column in another table. It also lets you create relations between tables. A foreign key in a table is always a primary key in another table. Foreign keys are used to enforce data integrity by being part of foreign key constraints. Foreign key constraints are created to make sure referential integrity is preserved and not violated. There are two foreign keys in the OrderDetail table. The first is the ProductID foreign key, and it's related to the primary key named ProductID in the Product table. The second is the OrderID foreign key, and it's related to the primary key named OrderID in the OrderHeader table. Concerning the naming of foreign keys, it's good practice to define them using the same name as their primary key counterpart; otherwise, it might lead to problems for people looking at your logical data model.

I introduced you to data integrity earlier in this chapter. When doing so, I cited an example that could create similar problems to the one in the Product and OrderDetail table example. Adding a foreign key constraint between these two tables would prevent a user from deleting a product in the Product table that could potentially create a large number of orphaned rows in the OrderDetail table. If you look at Figure 8-1, the foreign key constraint between Product and OrderDetail is shown as a line labeled FK_Product_OrderDetail between the two tables. Naming constraints is an easy way to understand their purpose. We have only three tables in our example, but you can imagine that constraints without names that exist between numerous tables would quickly become unclear.

Another foreign key constraint is the one between the OrderHeader and OrderDetail tables; this constraint prevents an order from being deleted before all of its matching order details have been deleted. You can see in Figure 8-1 that the OrderHeader table has a second foreign key called CustomerID. Therefore, another foreign key constraint is between the Customer and OrderHeader tables. Following the same principles found with other foreign key constraints, this prevents a customer in the Customer table from being deleted before all the matching orders in the OrderHeader table and all the detail rows in the OrderDetail table that match the orders have been deleted.

If there were no foreign key constraints in this database, data integrity would be easily violated. The database would be left with a big problem: a time bomb of orphaned rows that take up space and slow down all queries. By adding foreign key constraints, the RDBMS ensures, for example, that all rows in the OrderDetail table that reference a product have been deleted before the product row can be deleted in the Product table.

How Do You Interact with a Relational Database?

So far, I've talked about tables in which you can update, add, or delete rows or query the database to get particular results. Perhaps you've been asking yourself, "But how do I talk or interact with the database? How does it return the answers to my queries? And how do you create those tables?" I'm sure you've been asking yourself many other questions as well. The answer to all of these questions in this chapter is SQL Server 2005 Express Edition.

SQL stands for Structured Query Language and was invented in the 1970s. The acronym is pronounced "sequel" and was also introduced using that same spelling, but because of a trademark dispute in the United Kingdom in the 1970s, the name was shortened to the now well-known SQL acronym. (The other acronym, SEQUEL, means Structured English Query

Language.) SQL is an English-based language and is similar to human-language questions. That's why it's easy and fast to learn basic SQL programming. Let's look at two examples:

```
SELECT * FROM CUSTOMER
SELECT COUNT(*) FROM PRODUCT
```

The first line can be translated as give me all (*) rows in the Customer table, or (less formally) give me the list of customers. The second line can be translated as a request to give me the total of all rows contained in the Product table—in other words, to count how many products this company has.

When you issue a SQL query to a relational database, the database returns a result set that simply contains the rows with the answers to your query. Using SQL, you can also group or aggregate the results of a query. You also use SQL to create tables or delete (drop) tables. You've learned about primary keys, foreign keys, and constraints, but you probably didn't know that they're also created using SQL.

It's also good to know that SQL is an ANSI/ISO standard; therefore, any RDBMS producer needs to obey a set of rules. Basic SQL is a base programming language and as such is usually not sufficient to solve all the possible problems or provide all the analysis needs that an application might demand. It has a rather limited set of keywords. Because their first goal is to query data from a database, the most popular RDBMSs on the market have added extensions to SQL to permit the addition of procedural code. These additions turn SQL into a full-fledged programming language that helps solve more complex problems. Among the popular extensions and their manufacturers are Microsoft Transact-SQL (T-SQL), Oracle PL/SQL, and IBM SQL PL. Recently, in addition to these extensions, RDBMS manufacturers have added support for other programming languages. Microsoft added .NET language support into the database with all SQL Server 2005 editions, while Oracle and IBM have added Java support.

There are more database concepts and theories than those explained here, but I have covered the immediate database needs for this book. You'll now apply those concepts concretely in a Windows Forms application that will use a SQL Server Express 2005 database.

In this section, you will develop a Windows Forms application. This will be a car-tracking application that lets the user track the prices of cars over time and determine where the listing was observed. You will first use Visual Studio to create the database and the tables, and then you'll add some data and validate some of the concepts you just learned. You will then create a Windows application that will use your data and build a data-centric application that lets users store any amount of data.

Refer to Figure 8-2 for the database diagram pertaining to this section's example.

MORE INFO

SQL Server is well integrated because Visual Studio provides a great software development kit (SDK) for other components to plug into the IDE.

MORE INFO

The .mdf file extension is used by the SQL Server family of products. The .mdf file contains the entire database, which means all tables and other elements that exist in the database are located in this file. The only element that is not part of the .mdf file is the log information, which is in an .ldf file that is created whenever you create a database. You can see the .ldf file by clicking the Show All Files icon in Solution Explorer.

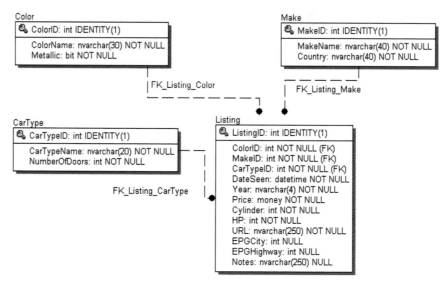

Figure 8-2
Car tracker application database diagram

Creating a Database Using Visual Basic 2008 Express Edition

Before using data, you need a place to store the data. In this section, you'll learn how to create a database in Visual Basic 2008 Express Edition. You'll also see how easy it is for you to create all the tables you need to satisfy the needs of the car-tracking application because the SQL Server team did a wonderful job of integrating the tools into Visual Studio.

TO CREATE A DATABASE USING VISUAL BASIC 2008 EXPRESS EDITION

1. Start Visual Basic 2008 Express Edition.

2. Create a new Windows Forms application, and name it CarTracker.

3. You will now create the database that will hold all the tables for the application. In Solution Explorer, right-click the CarTracker project, select Add, and then select New Item.

4. In the Add New Item dialog box, select Service-Based Database under Visual Studio Installed Templates. Type the filename **CarTracker.mdf**, and click the Add button. By doing so, you'll create a database and attach the database file (CarTracker.mdf) to your CarTracker project.

Figure 8-3
Solution Explorer with the newly created CarTracker. mdf database file

5. You will then see the Data Source Configuration Wizard. Don't pay attention to this dialog box just yet; you'll learn about it soon. Just click Cancel for now.

   Solution Explorer should now contain a new item within your project: the database file called CarTracker.mdf, as shown in Figure 8-3.

6. You will now start adding tables to your database. To do this, you can either double-click the CarTracker.mdf file or right-click CarTracker.mdf and then select Open. This causes Visual Studio to connect to the SQL Server 2005 Express Edition instance installed on your machine.

   Database Explorer should appear on the left side of the screen where the Toolbox usually opens, as shown in Figure 8-4. If you do not see Database Explorer, select the View menu, and then select Database Explorer.

   Under the database name, you should see a list of database elements represented by folder icons. Although you will not recognize most of them, you will see two elements

Figure 8-4
Database Explorer with the CarTracker database connected

that are already familiar to you: database diagrams and tables. You will use both of these elements shortly.

You'll know that you're connected to the database when you see the database icon with an electric cord. When you're disconnected, you will see the database icon with a red X. However, seeing a red X does not necessarily mean you're disconnected. You might have been disconnected earlier but never refreshed Database Explorer. To verify the state of the connection to your database, you should click the Refresh button in the Database Explorer toolbar.

7. Right-click your database named CarTracker.mdf in Database Explorer, and select Close Connection. You should now see the red X near your database name.

You're now disconnected. You can reconnect in a couple of ways. You can click the Refresh button, or you can right-click the filename in Database Explorer and select Modify Connection.... If you choose the Modify Connection route, you will see a dialog box like the one shown in Figure 8-5.

NOTE

Currently, you have only one database in your project, but it's not unusual to need to connect to and get information from two or more databases. That's why Database Connections in Database Explorer is there as a tree—it's representing each database as a node in that tree. You have only one node in the tree, which is your CarTracker database.

Figure 8-5
The Modify Connection dialog box lets you recon-nect to your CarTracker database.

8. Because it's good practice to test your connection, click the Test Connection button to verify the connection currently specified. This also verifies that SQL Server 2005 Express Edition is ready and able to receive connections from your applications. Click OK to reconnect to your database.

Creating Tables in Your Database

Now you'll create all the tables and relationships needed for the CarTracker application. Using the information found in Figure 8-2, you'll create tables, primary keys, identities, and foreign key relationships in the CarTracker database, and you'll do all of this without leaving Visual Studio.

TO CREATE TABLES IN A DATABASE

1. Let's start with the Color table. In Database Explorer, right-click the Tables folder icon, and select Add New Table. You should now see an empty grid on the designer surface, which is the Table Designer. You will also see that a new toolbar has appeared, which is the Table Designer toolbar. This toolbar has all the tools necessary to help you create a table without writing a single SQL query.

2. You'll now add a column to the Color table. Type **ColorID** in the Column Name field of the Table Designer. Select int as the data type, and clear the Allow Nulls check box because this column will be the primary key in this table. A primary key cannot be null since it is part of the uniqueness of a row in the table.

3. Before you add the second column in the Color table, you'll set the ColorID column as the primary key. To do so, you need to click the Set Primary Key icon (the key icon) in the Table Designer toolbar.

4. The database diagram shown in Figure 8-2 illustrates that you also need this column to be an identity; therefore, you need to modify that property in the Column Properties window right below the Table Designer. Scroll down until you see the Identity Specification group. Click the + sign located to the left of the words *Identity Specification* to expand this group. Now click in the (Is Identity) field, and set it to Yes. Leave both Identity Seed and Identity Increment set at 1 for now.

Saving Database Files

You should pay attention to the database filename in the Modify Connection dialog box. If you didn't save all the files in your project, everything is still located in a temporary folder identified by the content of the text box. As soon as you save all the files in your project, the database will be saved along with the other project files, wherever they are located. You can later verify that location by selecting the Tools menu, selecting Options..., and then looking at the Projects and Solutions node in the tree. On the right panel in this dialog box you can determine where your projects are stored by looking at the first text box called Visual Studio Projects Location.

NOTE

From this point onward, for every tree control and every control that is a group (that is, has a + sign), I'll use the word *expand* instead of repeating the words *click the + sign.*

NOTE

As a reminder, when a column is an identity, SQL Server automatically generates a new number each time a row is created in a table. It starts at the value indicated by the *Identity Seed* property and increases in increments by the value indicated by the *Identity Increment* property.

5. To add another column, click in the row under the ColorID column name. Add the two remaining columns based on the diagram shown in Figure 8-2. Set the size of the Color-Name nvarchar by typing **30** in the Data Type field. When done, your table should look like the one shown in Figure 8-6.

Figure 8-6
Table Designer with all the columns for the Color table

NOTE

In the Table Designer, the little black triangle indicates the current row.

6. Now that you're done with the design, you need to add the table to the database. To do this, you need to save the table. Click the Save icon, or press Ctrl+S. When the Choose Name dialog box appears, as shown in Figure 8-7, name your table Color, and then click OK.

Figure 8-7
The Choose Name dialog box showing the Color table name

Figure 8-8
Database Explorer with the Tables folder and Color table expanded

7. Expand the Tables folder in Database Explorer to view the list of existing tables in the database; the new Color table should appear. When you expand the Color table to view the list of columns, all three columns you just created should appear, as shown in Figure 8-8.

8. Close the Color table in the Table Designer by clicking the X near Solution Explorer.

9. Click the Save All icon in the toolbar to save your project on disk. Make sure the project name is CarTracker, and click the Save button.

10. Before creating other tables, read this step completely. Now that you have the knowledge to create a table, create all remaining tables (ColorType, Make, and Listing) using the same techniques you've just learned. Make sure all tables and all their columns are created in the same way as shown in Figure 8-2. Don't worry about establishing the relationships, because you'll create those in the following exercises. Between each table creation, save your new table immediately, and make sure it appears in Database Explorer. Then close the table in the designer surface as shown earlier in step 8 of this section.

Creating Relationships Between the Tables

You have created tables, but they don't have any relationships. You'll now add those relationships and make sure your database has data integrity to avoid any orphaned rows. Like many other elements in Visual Basic 2008 Express Edition, there's more than one way to create the relationships. One is more visual than the other, and you'll start with this more visual approach to stay focused on the main idea of the book, which is being productive.

Before you're able to create the relationships visually, there is a prerequisite to add to your project: a database diagram. It might not look exactly like the one shown in Figure 8-2, but it will be similar.

TO CREATE RELATIONSHIPS BETWEEN TABLES

1. Go to Database Explorer, and right-click the Database Diagrams node located above the Tables node. Select Add New Diagram. A dialog box appears indicating that SQL Server 2005 Express Edition doesn't have all the database objects it needs if you want to create database diagrams.

2. Click Yes to have SQL Server create the components it needs to obtain a database diagram. When it's done creating the components, you should be asked which tables you want to add to your diagram in the Add Table dialog box.

3. Select all the tables you created, and then click Add. It should take less than a minute for your diagram to appear. Click the Close button to indicate to Visual Studio that you have all the tables you need.

> **TIP**
> Whenever you click a column name in Database Explorer, you'll see the properties listed in the Properties window. This is the same Properties window you've been using, with one minor difference: it is a read-only view and therefore does not let you modify information.

> **TIP**
> Depending on your resolution, the view might be tight. If you want to view more of the diagram, you might need to unpin or close some windows, such as Solution Explorer or the Properties window; you can return these items to your screen by selecting the View menu and then selecting Solution Explorer or Properties Window. You can also change the zoom value by changing the value in the Zoom drop-down list.

4. Click the Save All button, or press Ctrl+Shift+S. You'll be asked to save your diagram and choose a name. Name your diagram CarTrackerDiagram.

5. If you don't see your database diagram, first go to the Database Diagrams node, expand it, and then open the diagram by double-clicking it. You should see the designer surface with all your tables.

    Let's focus on one relationship we need to create. When you look at Figure 8-2, you'll see that the ColorID column is present in the Listing table because there's a relationship to the Color table. The line between both tables is an FK relationship. You need to have this relationship established, or otherwise you'll have orphaned nodes in the Listing table whenever a Color row is deleted. This means you have to establish a relationship between the primary key table and the foreign key table. In this case, you need to create a relationship from the Color table toward the Listing table.

6. In the database diagram, click ColorID in the Color table where you see the small yellow key.

7. Look at Figure 8-9 to see where you should be at the end of this step. Drag ColorID toward the Listing table; you should see a line appear as you drag. Align your mouse pointer so that it's over the column with which you want to create the relationship—in your case, over the ColorID field in the Listing table. When you see a small + appear, drop it.

Figure 8-9
Creating the foreign key relationship between the Color and Listing tables

8. If you correctly selected and released the mouse button once you were over ColorID in the Listing table, you should see a Tables and Columns dialog box asking you to confirm the creation of the FK relationship. It's important for each table that ColorID is the column name that appears to link both tables in that dialog box. If the primary key and foreign key tables are correct and the selected column names are correct, click the OK button.

You should then see the Foreign Key Relationship dialog box shown in Figure 8-10.

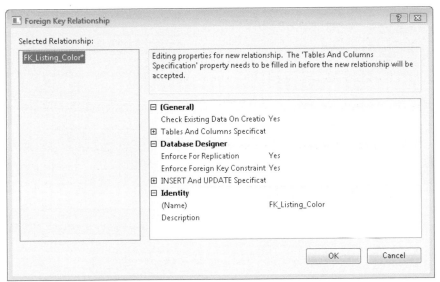

Figure 8-10
Foreign Key Relationship dialog box for the relationship between the Listing and Color tables

9. Although you can change some properties within this dialog box, just click OK for now. See Figure 8-11 to view the diagram with the new relationship created.

MORE INFO

To reinforce the concept of establishing relationships between tables, I'll now give you another way of looking at the relationship in this exercise. There are two reasons why the ColorID column is in the Listing table as an FK. First, it is used for a normalization and design principle because you don't want to have duplicate data. Second, it is used for data integrity reasons and, more specifically, for the orphaned rows problem. Let's look at it with some sample data. Suppose there is a Color row called Dark Blue, and the Listing table contains six different ad definitions that are Dark Blue. If you remove the Dark Blue color from the Color table, it would mean that those six ads would have orphaned data. That is why you created a foreign key relationship: to make sure that if an application or a user tries to remove data in the Color table, a process within SQL Server 2005 will prevent this by validating that no "kids" are left behind in the Listing table before allowing the deletion to occur in the Color table.

In Figure 8-11, note the infinity symbol located close to the Listing table and the yellow key located close to the Color table. The infinity symbol on the Listing table indicates the table's cardinality. It indicates that, in this relationship, the Listing table can contain any number of rows with information coming from the matching primary key table. The yellow key indicates from which table the primary key is being taken.

I rearranged the diagram so that the two tables are close together. You can rearrange your tables any way you want by dragging them by the title bar (that is, where the table name is displayed). This is sometimes necessary when you create relationships so that you do not end up with an unusual-looking diagram. I suggest you put your Listing table in the middle of your other tables because it will be easier to create relationships this way. You can also rearrange the tables on your diagram at any time by right-clicking anywhere except on a table on the diagram's designer surface and selecting Arrange Tables. You can also have the labels for every relationship appear on the diagram by right-clicking the diagram's designer surface and selecting Show Relationship Labels.

Now create the other FK relationships by using either Figure 8-2 or Table 8-4.

Figure 8-11
Modified diagram showing the new FK relationship between the Listing and Color tables

Column	Primary Key Table	Foreign Key Table
MakeID	Make	Listing
CarTypeID	CarType	Listing

Table 8-4
List of Foreign Key Relationships to Create

When finished, the content of your diagram should resemble the content shown in Figure 8-12. Make sure your relationships are arranged properly by looking at where the infinity symbols and yellow keys are located and by looking at Table 8-4 for verification.

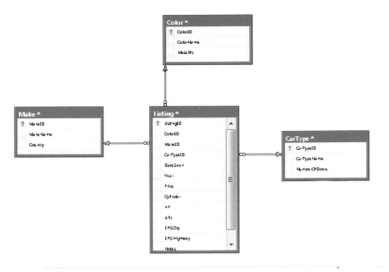

Figure 8-12
Completed CarTracker database diagram

MORE INFO

You can review the properties of any relationship by double-clicking the line between two tables or by right-clicking and selecting Properties from the context menu.

Click the Save All button or press Ctrl+Shift+S to commit the changes to the database. Click Yes when asked whether you want to save.

Entering Data in SQL Server Tables Using Visual Studio

Now that you have created all your tables and relationships, you'll start inserting data in your tables and verifying that your constraints ensure the data integrity of your database.

Let's start by adding data to all tables. You'll first add rows to the Color table.

TO ENTER DATA IN SQL SERVER TABLES USING VISUAL STUDIO

1. To start entering rows in the Color table, right-click the Color table in Database Explorer, and select Show Table Data. Your designer surface should have a grid like the one shown in Figure 8-13.

Entering Data

While typing your data, look to the table's leftmost area in the table data grid, and you'll see a small pencil icon, a star, or a small black triangle. The pencil indicates you're modifying the row. The star indicates a new row, and the small black triangle indicates the current row.

Figure 8-13
Empty Color table in the table data grid

2. Let's add the first color. Click the Color Name field, type **Dark Blue**, and then press the Tab key to go to the next column. Type **true** in the Metallic field. Because that column type is a bit, its values can be only either true or false because a bit type is a binary type. When you're done, press the Tab key to go to the next row.

Don't Add Data to Identity Columns

For all columns you created as identity columns, don't type the data because the field will automatically be generated by SQL Server 2005 Express Edition whenever the row is created in the table. If you try to type data in an identity column, you will not be allowed to do so. When the cursor is in an identity column, you'll see near the navigation bar at the bottom of the Table Designer that the cell is read-only.

3. Add three more car colors—Red, Silver, and Black—and set Red as Metallic and the other two colors as nonmetallic (that is, false). When you're done, the table should look like the one shown in Figure 8-14.

4. Add the data in Table 8-5 and Table 8-6 to the Make and CarType tables, respectively.

ColorID	ColorName	Metallic
1	Dark Blue	True
2	Red	True
3	Silver	False
4	Black	False
NULL	NULL	NULL

Figure 8-14
Color table with four new rows of data

MakeName	Country
GoodRoadster	Germany
SmallCar	France
BigSUV	USA
ReliableCar	Japan

Table 8-5
Data for the Make Table

CarTypeName	NumberOfDoors
Roadster	2
SUV	5
Hatchback	5
Sedan	4
Coupe	2

Table 8-6
Data for the CarType Table

You might not have realized that by giving a type to your data, you actually added data integrity verification to your database. Try modifying one of the Color rows by changing the Metallic column to *Helloworld* instead of *true* or *false*. You'll get an error message telling you that the Metallic field is of type Boolean.

To show how data integrity is preserved using the foreign key constraints, you'll add two Listing rows. You will enter more rows when using your Windows Forms application.

5. Right-click the Listing table, select Show Table Data, and add the two rows shown in Table 8-7.

MORE INFO
You can navigate through the table by using the navigation controls at the bottom of the grid. With these controls you can perform tasks such as moving to the first and last rows, moving to the previous and next entries, moving to a new record, or typing a row number to move to that row.

ColorID	MakeID	CarTypeID	DateSeen	Year	Price	Cylinder	HP	URL	EPGCity	EPGHighway	Notes
1	1	1	08/11/2008	2005	42500	6	240	http://www.litwareinc.com/	20	28	This is my dream car, follow regularly.
4	3	2	07/30/2008	2003	39775	8	340	http://www.cpandl.com/	10	15	Too much gas

Table 8-7
Data for the Listing Table

6. You'll now verify that one of your foreign key constraints is working correctly. Open the Make table by right-clicking the Make table and selecting Show Table Data.

7. Let's try to delete the first row by clicking the leftmost field where the pencil usually appears. The row should be selected, and all the fields should be blue. Right-click, and select Delete.

8. A dialog box should appear inquiring whether you really want to delete the row. Click Yes.

9. You should receive the following dialog box error message stating that the row was not deleted because of the foreign key constraint: "Error Message: The DELETE statement conflicted with the REFERENCE constraint 'FK_Listing_Make.'" This statement affirms why the foreign key constraint was created, which was to avoid orphaned rows. Figure 8-15 depicts what the error dialog box looks like and what kind of information is provided to help you debug the problem, if necessary. In this case, it's not a problem but a feature of your creation!

SQL and T-SQL Documentation

If you want more information about SQL and T-SQL, you can read the SQL Server 2005 Express Edition documentation at http://msdn2.microsoft.com/en-us/library/ms165706.aspx. The SQL Server 2005 Express Edition documentation is designed to help you answer most questions you might have, but it might also refer you to the SQL Server 2005 documentation. You can download the SQL Server 2005 documentation at http://msdn2.microsoft.com/en-us/sqlserver/bb428874.aspx.

Figure 8-15
Error dialog box showing the foreign key relationship preventing the deletion of a row from the Make table

10. Click OK to exit this dialog box.

11. Test your other constraints related to the Listing table by trying to delete the first row of the CarType table. You should receive the same error message.

Now that you have all your domain tables loaded with some data, you'll learn to use the database in a Windows Forms application. You'll learn about ADO.NET, about data binding with Windows Forms controls, and about LINQ.

What Are ADO.NET, Data Binding, and LINQ?

You rarely enter all data manually using Visual Studio. You typically let the user do it, or you do it through an application. You can also either import data from another source or create the new data using SQL scripts, but those are more advanced concepts that will not be covered in this book.

This section will focus on how to build Windows applications that can connect to and receive data from a SQL Server 2005 Express Edition database using ADO.NET and LINQ on datasets. The following is a formal, official definition of ADO.NET from the MSDN online library:

ADO.NET provides consistent access to data sources, such as Microsoft SQL Server, as well as data sources exposed through OLE DB and XML. Data-sharing consumer applications can use ADO.NET to connect to these data sources and retrieve, manipulate, and update data.

ADO.NET cleanly factors data access from data manipulation into discrete components that can be used separately or in tandem. ADO.NET includes .NET Framework data providers for connecting to a database, executing commands, and retrieving results. Those results are either processed directly or placed in an ADO.NET DataSet object in order to be exposed to the user in an ad-hoc manner, combined with data from multiple sources, or remoted between tiers. The ADO.NET DataSet object can also be used independently of a .NET Framework data provider to manage data local to the application or sourced from XML.

The ADO.NET classes are found in System.Data.dll and are integrated with the XML classes found in System.Xml.dll. When compiling code that uses the System.Data namespace, reference both System.Data.dll and System.Xml.dll.

I've presented the long and formal definition of ADO.NET because it contains elements you'll learn about while working with the CarTracker application. I also chose it because I want you to refer to it whenever you're working with ADO.NET. Here is a less formal definition that I think summarizes what ADO.NET is all about: ADO.NET is the .NET Framework way of accessing and programmatically manipulating databases or data using XML sources.

With ADO.NET 2.0 came new ways of accessing data from different sources. In Visual Basic 2008 Express Edition, you are limited to the following data sources: databases (SQL

> **NOTE**
>
> **Visual Basic 2008 Express Edition allows you to work with Microsoft Access databases, but working with SQL Server 2005 Express Edition gives you all the enterprise-quality benefits of SQL Server 2005, with the only downside being a reduced set of features.**

Server Express and Microsoft Access databases), Web services, and custom objects. It is much easier (that is, there is less code) to manipulate data in ADO.NET 2.0, especially when using all the tools included in Visual Studio 2008. Many new wizards and other tools make the experience of working with databases a pleasant one. Visual Studio 2008 covers numerous common scenarios with its tools and wizards, but it's also very powerful when used programmatically without using the visual tools. You will learn the basics in this book, but nothing is preventing you from learning more about data binding and ADO.NET and from unleashing powerful applications.

With LINQ you can create queries within your Visual Basic code and query and update all kinds of data (arrays, lists, XML, Web services, SQL databases) easily. Here's a formal definition of LINQ, and then let's jump into the code:

Language-Integrated Query (LINQ) adds query capabilities to Visual Basic and provides simple and powerful capabilities when you work with all kinds of data. Rather than sending a query to a database to be processed, or working with different query syntax for each type of data that you are searching, LINQ introduces queries as part of the Visual Basic language. It uses a unified syntax regardless of the type of data.

LINQ enables you to query data from a SQL Server database, XML, in-memory arrays and collections, ADO.NET datasets, or any other remote or local data source that supports LINQ. You can do all this with common Visual Basic language elements. Because your queries are written in the Visual Basic language, your query results are returned as strongly typed objects. These objects support IntelliSense, which enables you to write code faster and catch errors in your queries at compile time instead of at run time. LINQ queries can be used as the source of additional queries to refine results. They can also be bound to controls so that users can easily view and modify your query results.

We'll return to the topic of LINQ later in the implementation of the CarTracker application, but before proceeding any further, let's talk more about CarTracker. The main goal of the application is to track car ads over the Internet. Because you already have your database ready to go, you now need to consider what will be included in this application. What you need is simply a way of displaying the ads, adding new ads, modifying and deleting existing ads, and searching through the ads using a series of drop-down boxes that help you narrow your search based on certain criteria. These search criteria will come directly from the domain tables (in other words, separate drop-down controls for the car type, color, make, and so forth).

When using drop-down controls or any other controls with data that you know exists in your database, you don't want to populate the data by hand. You want to use the data-binding capabilities of a control. *Data binding* is an easy and transparent way to read and write data and link a control on a Windows form to a data source in your application.

NOTE
Not all Windows Forms controls are "data-binding-aware." When they are aware, they have a *DataBindings* property.

ADO.NET takes care of a great deal of activity behind the scenes (it's even better in .NET Framework 3.5), as well as managing the connection to the database. Managing the connection doesn't stop at opening and closing the connection; it also concerns itself with finding the database with which you're trying to connect. When a connection is opened, it means your application can talk to the database through ADO.NET method calls. ADO.NET manages all exchanges (send/receive) of data between your application and the database for you. ADO.NET also manages the data through diverse mechanisms: read-only forward navigation, navigation in any direction with read-write, field evaluation, and so forth. And the beauty of it is that you usually don't have to write a lot of code to enjoy those nice features.

Developing the CarTracker Application

You'll now start developing the CarTracker application. First you need to create a dataset that will provide you with all the data binding you need for the CarTracker application. Now that your tables are established, you can configure the dataset with all the elements you've just added to your database.

Before creating a dataset, though, you must learn what a dataset is. A *dataset* is an in-memory representation of one or more tables and is used to store the rows you retrieve that match the query you sent to the database. You can then add, delete, or update rows in memory. When the user is done, you can submit, save, or commit the changes to the database. In a few steps, you'll see the CarTrackerDataSet.xsd file, which is called an *XML schema definition* file. The .xsd file ensures that the data will be structured and respect the schema. You'll use this file later in the project when I discuss data binding.

Figure 8-16
The Data Sources window

To create a dataset, you'll learn to use the Data Sources window. This window gives you access to all the data sources you have configured in your application. Figure 8-16 shows where the Data Sources window is located. If you don't see the Data Sources window, you can access it by clicking the Data menu and clicking Show Data Sources. If Show Data Sources does not appear on the Data menu, be sure you have closed all the CarTracker table data grids and Form1 is visible.

NOTE
The Data Sources window might end up somewhere else in your IDE. Because your IDE is entirely customizable to your liking, you can have your windows and tabs appear wherever you think they are most productive for you.

TO CREATE A DATASET

1. In the Data Sources window, click the Add New Data Source link, or click the Add New Data Source button in the toolbar. The Data Source Configuration Wizard appears.

2. The first page of the Data Source Configuration Wizard prompts you to choose the data source type you want to create. You can choose a database, a Web service, or one of your objects. You've just built a database for the CarTracker application, so choose that data source type. Select Database, and then click Next.

3. On the next page, you will choose your data connection. You should see the CarTracker connection string prepopulating the Connection field. The reason is simple: when you created the CarTracker SQL Server Express Edition database in your project, a data connection was created for you. The connection string was added to your application as an application setting. (If you right-click your project name and select Properties and then the Settings tab, you will see the connection string entry. You can also expand the bottom of the dialog box to see what the connection string looks like.) This connection string defines how your application will connect to the database. Having the connection string in your application configuration file is actually a best practice. It gives you the advantage of only modifying the file and restarting the application without recompilation so as to automatically pick up the changes in your connection string and connect to that new location.

   The application configuration is stored in an XML file named using the application's executable name with .config added at the end of the executable filename. In our application, the file is named CarTracker.exe.config, although you see only app.config while working in Visual Studio.

4. Click Next on the Choose Your Data Connection page.

5. On the next page, you'll select all the tables from the database that will be in your dataset, and you'll name your dataset. In your case, you will need all the tables, so expand the Tables node, and select all the tables. Leave the dataset name set to CarTrackerDataSet, and then click Finish.

   The result of your dataset configuration is an .xsd file, or an XML schema document, and it will define the internal structure of your dataset. Remember that a dataset is an in-memory representation of one or more tables from your database. ADO.NET will use this schema file when working with your application. When running the application, the user will be able to add, delete, or modify rows in the dataset (in the computer's memory). The changes will remain in memory until the user commits the changes to the database, which in our example is the CarTracker.mdf file.

6. In Solution Explorer, double-click the .xsd file named CarTrackerDataSet.xsd. As shown in Figure 8-17, the result of the dataset creation is similar to the database diagram you created earlier. Your diagram might be different depending on your screen resolution and how you customized your IDE.

Figure 8-17
Graphical representation of the CarTracker dataset

There are some notable differences, however. You'll see the same columns you have created in your physical database, but at the bottom of each table you will see some methods: *Fill* and *GetData()*. These methods are particular to the dataset, and the

Figure 8-18
*View of the Color and Listing
dataset tables in the Data Sources
window*

ADO.NET-generated code by Visual Studio will use them to bind data to your Windows Forms controls—controls that do not exist yet!

7. Return to the Data Sources window, and expand the dataset tables. You'll see the in-memory representation of your tables, and you'll also see that each column has a small icon that gives you its type. These icons might look familiar to you because they are similar to the controls in the Toolbox. Refer to Figure 8-18 for a quick glance at the Color and Listing dataset tables and their column types.

8. Close the graphical representation of your dataset by clicking the X in the corner of the designer surface. Depending on your screen resolution, you might have moved the boxes around; if that's the case, when you try to close this window, you'll be asked to save it. You can click Yes if you want to preserve where on the design surface the data tables are located. This is only design-time information that will be saved because you didn't change anything else.

9. In Solution Explorer, double-click your Form1.vb file to open the designer surface for Form1.

10. In the Data Sources window, select the Listing node in your dataset, and click the drop-down arrow that's next to the word *Listing*. You will see two choices: DataGridView and Details. DataGridView brings all the dataset fields into a table or grid format with multiple rows, while Details brings the dataset fields in one row at a time with all fields as individual controls. For our example, select Details.

You'll also see that each member of the dataset has the same drop-down arrow, which means you can change which controls will be dropped onto the form when it is dragged. Choosing controls prior to dragging the dataset table onto the form prevents you from having to lay out the UI piece by piece.

11. Change ColorID, MakeID, and CarTypeID to the ComboBox type by clicking the drop-down arrow next to each column and selecting ComboBox.

12. Select the Listing node by clicking it, and then drag it near the top-left corner of the designer surface on Form1.

13. You'll now modify the form size like you did in previous chapters by modifying the form's *Size* property. Change the form size so that its width is 450 pixels and its height is 550 pixels.

14. Move all the controls so that the first label is almost in the top-left corner just beneath the tool strip. See Figure 8-19 to determine how the controls should approximately be placed.

CAUTION
You may need to scroll to see all the controls depending on your screen resolution.

Figure 8-19
Resized CarTracker form after moving all the controls

As you can see, many things have just happened. Let's start by looking at the designer surface. All the fields from the dataset have been added as controls, and labels were also added based on the name of the field in the dataset. This feature is called Smart Captions. Visual Studio uses Pascal or camel casing as a mechanism to insert a space in labels when using Smart Captions. When you drop the dataset fields onto the form, the Smart Captions feature looks at each field's casing. When it finds an uppercase letter or an underscore (_) character following a lowercase letter, it inserts or replaces the underscore with a space. You can see an exception to this rule in the EPGCity and EPGHighway fields. When you use uppercase letters for an acronym, for example, Visual Studio cannot distinguish that these are two words and therefore doesn't split them apart. You'll have to split these two fields manually.

Know Your Files

When working with local database files, understand that they are treated like any other content file. For desktop projects, this means that by default the database file will be copied to the output folder (that is, bin) each time the project is built. After pressing F5, here's what your file structure will look like on disk:

CarTracker\CarTracker.mdf

CarTracker\Form1.vb

CarTracker\Bin\Debug\CarTracker.mdf

CarTracker\Bin\Debug\CarTracker.exe

At design time, the data tools and wizards use CarTracker\CarTracker.mdf. At run time, the application uses the database under the bin\debug folder. As a result of the copy operation, many people assume the application did not save the data to the database file because two copies of the data file are involved. This also happens when looking at schema/data through Database Explorer. The tools are using the copy in the project folder and not the file in the bin\debug folder.

The following are a few ways to work around this copy behavior.

First, if you select your database file in Solution Explorer, you will see a property called Copy to Output Directory *in the Properties window. By default, it is set to* Copy Always, *which means data files in the project folder will be copied to the bin\debug folder on each build, thus overwriting the existing data files, if any. You can set this property to* Do Not Copy *and then manually place a copy of the data file in the bin\debug folder. In this way, on subsequent builds, the project system leaves the database file in the bin\debug folder and doesn't try to overwrite it with the one from the project. The downside to this method is that you still have two copies. Therefore, after you modify the database file using the application, if you want to make those same changes within the project, you need to copy the changes to the project manually, and vice versa.*

The other approach is to leave the data file outside the project and create a connection to it in Database Explorer. When the IDE asks you to bring the file into the project, simply click No. This way, both the design time and the run time will be using the same data file. The downside to this method is that the path in the connection string will be hard-coded, and it will therefore be harder to share the project and deploy the application. Before deploying the application, make sure to replace the full path in the settings with a relative path. If you want to read more about the relative path versus the full path (plus a bit more about this copy behavior), read the following article: http://blogs.msdn.com/smartclientdata/archive/2005/08/26/456886.aspx. You'll see that I took portions of that article and modified them so that they fit our application.

Microsoft Visual Basic 2008 Express Edition: Build a Program Now!

You will also notice that a tool strip has been added that contains almost the same buttons you used while working with the database Table Designer.

15. Read the "Know Your Files" sidebar on the previous page. With this copy behavior in mind, I suggest you use the first approach even though you'll have to perform some manual steps. If you want to debug your application from within Visual Studio, it's preferable to use this solution, or you will not be able to see the changes applied to your database file. The database file will always return to the initial one from your project, which is similar to resetting the whole database to what it is in Visual Studio.

16. Select the CarTracker.mdf database file in Solution Explorer, and change the *Copy to Output Directory* property to *Do Not Copy* in the Properties window.

17. Press F5 to build and run your application. You'll get an exception message because the file won't be copied in the bin\debug directory. Also, on the form load event when your code tries to fill the dataset, it won't find the database at the place specified by the connection string. Therefore, you get a SQLException stating that it's not able to attach to the database. Click the Stop Debugging button or press Shift+F5 to stop debugging.

18. Using Windows Explorer, go into your project directory (it should be located at Users\<yourusername>\Documents\Visual Studio 2008\ Projects\CarTracker\CarTracker\), and copy the .mdf and .ldf files into the bin\debug directory under CarTracker. If you're not able to copy the files because Visual Studio still has them open, save all your files, and then close the project. Then copy the two files mentioned earlier, and re-open your project.

19. Now press F5 to build and run your application again.

You should see the two records you've manually inserted into the Listing table. You should be able to navigate using the tool strip and also modify, insert, and delete a record. Figure 8-20 shows a snapshot of your CarTracker application at run time.

20. Change the URL of the row at position 1 to end with .net instead of .com.

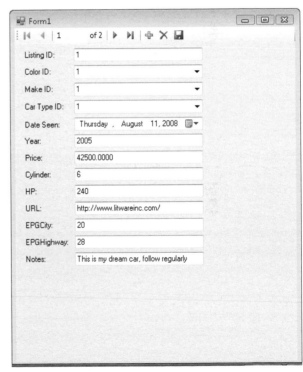

Figure 8-20
Execution of the CarTracker application

NOTE

If you want the same data in Visual Studio as you have when executing the application in debug mode, you must close your project completely. Using Windows Explorer, copy the .mdf and .ldf files from the bin\debug folder to the project folder. When you reopen your project, the database will now contain the same content.

Suppose you then want to modify the structure of your database, such as adding a column to a table. If you don't want to lose the data within the bin\debug database files, you must copy them to the project folder before you modify the table structure. When done with the modifications, you simply copy both the .mdf and .ldf files back to the bin\debug folder. Of course, if your application needs those new database changes, you will also have to modify the dataset, but that process is beyond the scope of this book.

21. After changing the URL for the record, click the disk icon to commit the changes to the database.

22. Close the CarTracker application, and restart it by pressing F5. You should now see the first row with the modified URL ending in .net. Close the application again.

23. To verify that you are working with design-time and run-time versions of the CarTracker database, open the Listing table, and select Show Table Data in Database Explorer. The first row should still contain a URL column ending in .com and not in .net.

Point proven! The database file in Visual Studio is now decoupled from the one your application is using at run time. Read the note in the left margin to learn how to make the data the same in both the design-time and run-time versions.

Using the Component Tray

When you dragged the Listing dataset table to the designer surface, you probably saw that five items were added in the gray area below the designer surface. This section of the designer surface is called the *component tray* and is the section Visual Studio uses for nonvisual controls. In your case, it added an instance of the CarTracker dataset, a Listing table adapter, a Listing binding source, a table adapter manager, and finally a Listing binding navigator.

I'll describe several of these individually:

■ **Binding source**   You can think of a binding source as a "broker" or a layer of indirection. You can also think of it as an intermediary between a data-bound control on your form and a data source, such as a dataset. A binding source provides currency management and notification services (events). The binding source has many methods to facilitate, such as sorting, filtering, navigating, and editing of data from its data-bound controls to the data source. It's also linked tightly to the next component: the binding navigator. When you see a binding navigator, you're assured of getting a binding source.

■ **Binding navigator**   The binding navigator is a means to add navigation and data manipulation. It has a UI component or, more specifically, a tool strip with buttons to facilitate the functionality provided by the binding source.

■ **Typed dataset**   Although you know what a dataset is, you might not know that it's a strongly typed object. It contains data tables of the *DataTable* type that constitute the in-memory representation of your database tables. These data tables also have a special data adapter called the *table adapter*. There is a table adapter for each data table.

- **Table adapter**   A table adapter is a data access object. It connects to the database (for example, SQL Server 2005 Express Edition), executes the queries, and fills a data table with data when it returns from SQL Server. Therefore, it's the central point for all data access on an individual table. There is one table adapter per table in your data source. A table adapter can have more than one SELECT query.

- **Table adapter manager**   The *TableAdapterManager* class has been added in .NET 3.5 to help you maintain referential integrity to your typed datasets. It adds logic to maintain it and lets you specify in which order the CRUD (create, read, update, delete) transactions are happening. For instance, you can say that the update order is insert-update-delete or update-insert-delete. It also helps you to have a single point of update, so instead of calling the update method on each table adapter, you just have to call the *TableAdapater-Manager.UpdateAll* method to save the changes to the database.

How Do I Get More Meaningful Information on My Form?

Let's return to our CarTracker project. As you can see when you run the application, the ColorID, MakeID, and CarTypeID combo boxes are there, but they are displaying the ID and not the name associated with the ID. This is not helpful for the user because an ID doesn't have any meaning to users, and they might not be able to easily add or modify rows without having a human-readable format for those columns. Consequently, you need to make sure the data is displayed in a humanly readable way and that the ID is stored in the row whenever the user modifies the information.

There's an easy way to accomplish this, which you will do now for your three combo boxes.

TO DATA BIND WITH DOMAIN TABLES

1. In the Data Sources window, select the Color table from the dataset, drag it onto the form's designer surface over the ColorID combo box, and drop it.

ComboBox Tasks

☑ Use data bound items

Data Binding Mode

Data Source	ColorBindingSource ▾
Display Member	ColorName ▾
Value Member	ColorID ▾
Selected Value	ListingBindingSource - (▾

Add Query...

Preview Data...

Figure 8-21
ColorID combo box Smart Tag infor-
mation showing the Data Binding
Mode information box

MORE INFO

This intelligent data binding is a
Visual Studio feature called Smart
Defaults. Smart Defaults looks in
the dataset table to see whether
there's a column of type string by
either the ID or the primary key.
If so, it tries to use this one for
the data binding.

You'll see that another table adapter (ColorTableAdapter) and another binding source (ColorBindingSource) were added to the component tray. If you go to the ColorID combo box and click the Smart Tag triangle, you'll see the Data Binding Mode information box appear, as shown in Figure 8-21. You'll notice that your drag-and-drop action bound the combo box control with the ColorBindingSource. Because of this action, whenever the combo box is displayed, it will show the color names instead of ColorID. When the user picks a color from the combo box, the associated value member that will be used in the row will still be the ColorID, specifically the ColorID associated with the ColorName. Wonderful, isn't it? And we didn't use any lines of code.

2. Repeat the same process for the Make and CarType dataset tables and the corresponding MakeID and CarTypeID combo boxes.

3. Build and run your application, and then look at each combo box. You now have real color names and not merely ColorIDs; the same is true for CarType and Make. The combo boxes are also populated with all the values coming from those tables and not simply the value for that specific row. Click the down arrow, and you'll see all other potential values. Close the application.

4. On the form, remove the *ID* part from the ColorID, MakeID, and CarTypeID labels.

5. You will now enlarge the Notes field by making it a multiline text box. Select the Notes text box, and change the *Multiline* property to *true*. Also change the *MaxLength* property to *250*, the *Size:Height* property to *50*, and the *Size:Width* property to *250*.

6. Delete the ListingID text box and its label.

7. Size and reposition the controls on the form so that the form resembles the one shown in Figure 8-22; it does not need to be an exact duplicate. It will be good practice to bring back UI design concepts from Chapter 5, "Using Rapid Application Development Tools with Visual Basic 2008," and also good preparation for Chapter 9, "Building Your Own Weather Tracker Application." Change the *Text* property of the form to *Car Tracker*.

8. In Solution Explorer, rename form1.vb to Main.vb.

Figure 8-22
New visual aspects of the CarTracker application

9. Select the form, and change the *BackColor* property to *GradientActiveCaption*.

10. Now add a tool strip container to the form like you did in Chapter 6, "Modifying Your Web Browser." Set the *Dock* property to fill the form. In the Smart Tag menu, select Re-Parent Controls to place all your tool strips on the top panel and all your other controls in your content panel. If necessary, use the Document Outline window to view and adjust the hierarchy of objects on the form.

Everything is nearly complete for this application, but the research capabilities are lacking. Currently, the only way to search is to scan through all the rows until you find the correct one. This is not difficult now because you have only two rows in your CarTracker database. Yet, if you had 500 rows, the Scan method would not be effective at all! Therefore, you'll implement search capabilities by adding queries to your application by using the Dataset Designer. That's where we will introduce the LINQ to Datasets capabilities. You will do one search capability with plain ADO.NET and two with LINQ to Datasets. After that, you will add a bit more functionality to your application using LINQ.

TO ADD QUERIES TO YOUR APPLICATION

1. Let's start by adding the search capability to our application by using ADO.NET. In the Data Sources window, select CarTrackerDataSet. Right-click, and select Edit DataSet with Designer.

2. Select the Listing data table, and then select the ListingTableAdapter section at the bottom of the data table.

   When you look at the Properties window, you'll see that four types of queries were automatically generated by Visual Studio: SelectCommand, InsertCommand, DeleteCommand, and UpdateCommand. They are the queries that help you have a fully workable application without writing a single line of code. When you read about table adapters earlier, you learned that you can have multiple queries with a table adapter because it is the central point of data access. You will thus add search capabilities to your application by adding queries to the table adapters and by using elements from the UI as parameters to your queries. You will first add the ability to search for listings that have a certain color.

3. Right-click the ListingTableAdapter section, and select Add Query..., as shown in Figure 8-23.

   This brings you to the TableAdapter Query Configuration Wizard. This wizard will help you add another SELECT query that will use parameters to refine your search. You can also create a SELECT query and turn it into a stored procedure or use an existing stored procedure. As its name implies, a *stored procedure* is stored in SQL Server and contains SQL statements, along with other programming constructs, that use T-SQL.

   A new feature in SQL Server 2005 Express Edition is that stored procedures can also be coded in managed languages, such as C# and Visual Basic. Stored procedures are executed on the server. This approach is usually considered safer because no SQL code is included in your application and everything executes on a separate machine, usually in a different physical location. It used to be a bit more performant, but with the newest ADO.NET, the performance argument is not as big as the safety argument. Since you're using SQL Server 2005 Express Edition, this will be of no concern because SQL Server and the application are executed on the same machine.

Figure 8-23
Adding new queries to a table adapter

4. Select Use SQL Statements, and click Next. When asked which type of SQL query you want to use, choose SELECT Which Return Rows, and then click Next. Note that you could have added any SQL query type you wanted.

5. You are now presented with an edit window in which to add the SQL statement that will perform a search for all the listings containing a particular color. Refer to Figure 8-24 to see the SQL command edit window. Click the Query Builder... button to get a visual view of the query.

Figure 8-24
SQL command edit window ready to customize the user's search

6. You will now add the Color table to the diagram so that you'll be able to base your search on a particular color. To add the Color table, simply right-click in the diagram area, and select Add Table.... The Add Table dialog box appears, as shown in Figure 8-25. Select

the Color table, and click the Add button. When the Color table has been added to the diagram, click the Close button.

Figure 8-25
The Add Table dialog box

MORE INFO

The % symbol is the wildcard character in SQL, and it can mean anything. For example, in the previous WHERE clause, it means return something that has a color similar to the *colorname* parameter.

7. In the SQL code pane of Query Builder, append the following SQL code that will help in the filtering process:

```
WHERE     (Color.ColorName LIKE '%' + @colorname + '%')
```

8. Before you proceed with your new query, make sure it will give you the results you're expecting. Click the Execute Query button to display the Query Parameters dialog box, as shown in Figure 8-26.

Figure 8-26
Query Parameters dialog box with prompt to enter a color name value

9. Try replacing the word *NULL* with *blue*, and then click OK. The Results pane of Query Builder should display only one row. Using the word *black* should return the black car row. Simply enter **b**, and you should get both the blue and the black rows. Once you're satisfied with your query, click OK in Query Builder.

10. On the Specify a SQL SELECT Statement page of the wizard, click Next. It's time to add your query to the application.

11. A page appears that prompts you to name the methods that your query will generate. After you create the query, those methods will be available from the Listing table adapter. Refer to Figure 8-27 to view this screen, which contains the two new method names. For both names you basically need to add what your filter is. In your case, you can add ColorName since you filtered by that name in your WHERE clause. When done, click Next.

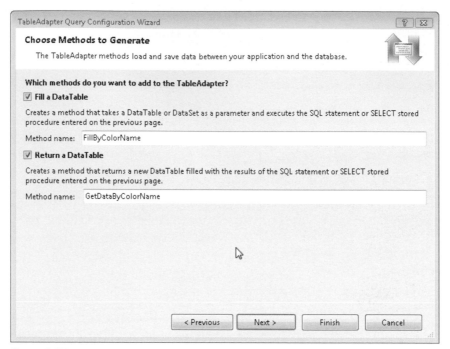

Figure 8-27
Use this page of the Query Configuration Wizard to rename the methods used to increase search capabilities.

12. After processing for a few seconds, your computer should come back with a results page informing you that your SELECT statement and your new *Fill* and *Get* methods are ready to use. Click the Finish button.

   Look at the table adapter section of the Listing data table. Your new methods will be added there.

13. In Solution Explorer, double-click Main.vb. Go to the component tray, click the Listing-TableAdapter Smart Tag, and select Add Query.... You'll see a Search Criteria Builder dialog box that will prompt you to create a new query or pick an existing one. Since you just built a new method, you merely need to select one. Select the Existing Query Name option, and then select FillByColorName, as shown in Figure 8-28.

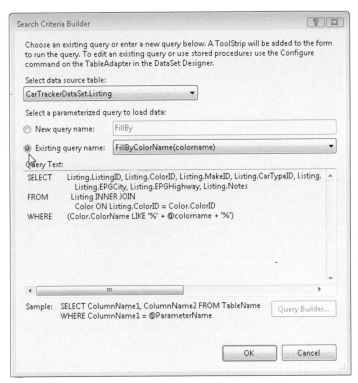

Figure 8-28
Search Criteria Builder with the FillByColorName *method selected*

14. Click the OK button. You'll see that a tool strip has been placed at the top of the form with a search button that will call your method when you click it, thereby giving you a way of searching by certain criteria. This was accomplished by typing only the WHERE clause for your specific query.

15. Extend the top panel by clicking the grip and pulling it down so that it becomes two tool strips wide.

16. Make sure your application looks like the one shown in Figure 8-29. Press F5 to see the results of your work. Type **blue** in the ColorName tool strip, and click FillByColorName to see whether it returns blue color car listings.

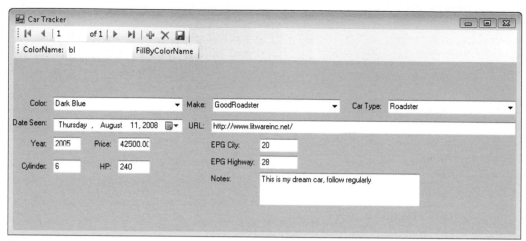

Figure 8-29
CarTracker application screen with the filter by color name

17. You will now add the two other buttons to the tool strip to narrow down the number of rows: one for the car type and one for the make. Add two tool strip labels, two tool strip text boxes, and two tool strip buttons. You can find the magnifier image in the Chapter6 folder of the companion content. Set the *Image* property to the file by browsing to that Images folder in Chapter6. Figure 8-30 shows what you should have when you're done. Make sure to name your variables appropriately because you'll need them in the event handlers in a minute.

Figure 8-30
Tool strip after you're done adding Filter By Make and Filter By CarType

Using LINQ

How you use LINQ depends on the type of data you are playing with. When used with strongly typed datasets (the ones we have), LINQ queries in code almost look like SQL. Let's look at the structure of a query using LINQ. MSDN states that a LINQ query, often referred to as a *query expression*, consists of a combination of query clauses identifying the data sources and iteration variables for the query. A query expression can also include instructions for sorting, filtering, grouping, and joining or can include calculations to apply to the source data. Query expression syntax resembles the syntax of SQL; therefore, you might find much of the syntax familiar. The following query gives us the customer names for all customers who are in the United States:

```
Dim queryResults = From cust In customers _
    Where cust.Country = "USA"
    Select cust.CompanyName, cust.Country
```

Now we'll use LINQ in CarTracker.

TO USE A LINQ QUERY

1. Double-click the tool strip button for the Make filter, and insert the following code:

```
Dim filteredByMake = From Listing In Me.CarTrackerDataSet.Listing _
                     Join Make In Me.CarTrackerDataSet.Make _
                     On Listing.MakeID Equals Make.MakeID _
                     Where Make.MakeName.ToLower() Like _
                     "*" & Me.tstbFilterByMake.Text.ToLower() & "*" _
                     Select Listing

Me.ListingBindingSource.DataSource = filteredByMake
```

This is essentially the same step you performed for the color filtering, except you didn't add a query to the dataset; instead, you used LINQ to filter the results on the screen. In reality, the dataset in memory still contains all the data, but you are displaying only the rows that match one of your filters. That's nice!

I'll now explain what is happening. The LINQ query you just wrote is joining two tables in your CarTracker dataset on the MakeID column and is also using the value in the tool strip text box for comparison. Note that *Like* is very similar to the use of LIKE in the color filter, except that the syntax is slightly different for the wildcard. Finally, you can assign the result of your query (in other words, *filteredByMake*) to the *DataSource* property of your binding source because it is a collection of Listing rows. Therefore you can simply assign it to the data source in the same way you would do it without LINQ.

2. Now let's do the same for CarType by adding the following code to the *Click* event of the tool strip button for the Filter By CarType text box:

```
Dim filteredByCarType = From Listing In Me.CarTrackerDataSet.Listing _
                        Join CarType In Me.CarTrackerDataSet.CarType _
                        On Listing.CarTypeID Equals CarType.CarTypeID _
                        Where CarType.CarTypeName.ToLower() Like _
                        "*" & Me.tstbFilterByCarType.Text.ToLower() & "*" _
                        Select Listing

Me.ListingBindingSource.DataSource = filteredByCarType
```

Figure 8-31 shows what you should have at the end of this chapter.

Figure 8-31
CarTracker application with all the filters

Test the application by adding new rows of data that have similar Make and CarType values and colors so you can validate that your application works well. Note that you could have created the same application by using LINQ to SQL. This book won't go into the details of the implementation for LINQ to SQL, but if you want to learn more about it, please take a look at the free video series at this Web site: *http://www.myvbprof.com/2007_Version/LINQ_to_SQL.aspx*. You'll see that there are many similarities to what we have done in this chapter. On the same Web site, you'll find another great video series talking about programming with XML in Visual Basic 2008. You'll find another use of LINQ called LINQ to XML. Just note that with LINQ you can use the query structure on many different collections of data. For example, you could do a LINQ query on strings in a dictionary and then iterate through the result with a *For Each* loop. LINQ is a wonderful and powerful new technology that will save you time and lines of code and that will improve the readability of your code.

CarTracker is a simple application that you can probably modify to handle more information, such as pictures of the cars. But there is nothing you can't add by yourself now! Here's a list of other tasks you can perform if you want to continue to work on this application:

- Add validations for user input, such as making sure the year of the car is not greater than the current year + 2.
- Add pictures in the databases and on the form.
- Add a sold check mark.
- Add three forms to add data in the domain tables (CarType, Make, Color).
- Add more information in the listing, such as contact information.
- Make the URL clickable.
- Save an ad as a text file.

In Summary...

That was a big chapter with a lot of material! Let's review what you've learned. You were first introduced to databases and database concepts. You learned what constitutes a database and what you usually find within a database. You learned about data integrity and how it relates to primary keys and foreign keys.

You then used Visual Basic 2008 Express Edition to create a database and tables and then populated them with some initial data using various tools in Visual Basic 2008 Express Edition. You implemented all the foreign key relationships without leaving Visual Studio and validated them as well.

After entering your data manually, you developed a sample CarTracker application that lets a user easily enter data and that uses ADO.NET and data binding.

Lastly, you learned about the new components of ADO.NET 2.0 and how, with little or no code, you can develop a fully working data-centric application. You've been introduced only to a brief part of ADO.NET, because it's a vast subject. If you want to learn more, refer to the code or samples on MSDN. A good place to begin is the samples for Visual Studio 2008. Pay particular attention to the topic of data access with ADO.NET and LINQ. Here's the link: *http://msdn2.microsoft.com/en-us/vbasic/bb466226.aspx?wt.slv=RightRail*. Also refer to the Windows Forms videos at the following link: *http://windowsclient.net/learn/videos.aspx*. At this location you'll find some data binding examples. Finally, look at the Learn Visual Basic Web site; this site evolves over time and will provide you with additional sources for learning data access using Visual Basic: *http://msdn2.microsoft.com/en-us/vbasic/ms789086.aspx?wt.slv=RightRail*.

In the next chapter, you will develop the final application of this book—the Weather Tracker application. You'll learn new concepts such as deployment, consuming Web services, user settings, and much more in a complete application with all the necessary validations.

Chapter 9

Building Your Own Weather Tracker Application

You have now reached the last chapter of the book and have learned quite a few new concepts along the way. In this chapter, you'll dot the i's and cross the t's by developing a fully functional weather-tracking application. You will be working with new processes in this chapter, but you will also draw on what you've learned in previous chapters to create the final product. In this chapter, you will put everything you've learned together to create this one application.

In this section, you'll become acquainted with the features used to create version 1.0 of the weather-tracking application, called Weather Tracker. This application contains the following features in version 1.0:

- Starts and resides as an icon in the notification area.
- Configures optional user settings from the notification area icon in the context menu.
- Refreshes all weather data on demand from the context menu in the notification area.
- Uses the MSN Weather service to provide data (weather locations, conditions, and forecasts) for cities around the world.
- Stores and persists user settings using XML.
- Minimizes but doesn't close when the user clicks the Close button in the title bar. The application will close only when the user clicks Exit on the context menu.
- Contains a splash screen on start-up.
- Contains an About box available from the context menu.
- Displays the current temperature in the system tray with a weather icon and color coding.
- Converts between metric units and English (or Imperial) units.

The application will not contain the following features in version 1.0:

- Will not work for more than one city at a time
- No graphical gauge controls for wind, pressure, temperature, and so forth

I'll now explain how the Weather Tracker application functions. First, the user will briefly see the splash screen. Then the application will go directly to the notification area in the Windows taskbar and display the current temperature. If the temperature is above 100 degrees Fahrenheit (or 38 degrees Celsius), the temperature will be displayed in red starting at 00. If the temperature is below 32 degrees Fahrenheit (or 0 degrees Celsius, which are negative degrees), the temperature will be displayed in violet. If the temperature in Fahrenheit is below 0 (or -18 degrees Celsius), the temperature will be displayed in blue. Otherwise, the temperature will be displayed in white. If the reading is not complete, a red *NA* will show up in place of the temperature reading.

If the user right-clicks the icon in the notification area, a context menu opens with choices to open the Main form and retrieve the current weather. The current weather will have an icon and provide useful weather data that comes from the MSN Weather service.

Clicking Refresh Weather Info in the context menu after clicking the notification area icon will trigger a call to the weather Web service to update weather data. This will be done asynchronously and will start by updating the current weather. If the user clicks Options in the context menu, an Options dialog box will be displayed. The user will be able to search for different cities around the world. If the user clicks About in the context menu, the application will display an About dialog box.

In this chapter, I will use a different approach than in previous chapters. Specifically, as long as you are using the same components that I specify, you can personalize your application as far as size, color, and other attributes are concerned. I'll also present my solution at different steps in the development; therefore, if you like what you see, you can proceed with your application by using the companion content that's provided. I will also present a great deal of code and explain the sections that are linked to the features described earlier.

To produce the application in this chapter, you will follow an incremental approach in which you implement one feature, integrate it with the rest of the application, and then test it. You will then move to the next feature until the application is complete.

Creating the Application User Interface

The Main form user interface (UI) will contain all the weather information you'll display to the user. Figure 9-1 shows what the Main form will look like when finished.

NOTE

As you learned in the previous chapter, you use data binding to bind the controls to the weather data. You'll recall that when creating the data source, you had a choice of Database, Web Service, and Objects. In this application, you will use a Web service as a data source, and the fields you will display on the form will be data bound to the Web service dataset.

IMPORTANT

All icons or image files in this chapter are in a folder named Images under the Chapter9 folder where you installed the companion content. The default location is Documents\Microsoft Press\VB 2008 Express\.

Figure 9-1
Main form in the Weather Tracker application

TO CREATE A DATA SOURCE FOR A MAIN FORM CONTROL

1. Start Microsoft Visual Basic 2008 Express Edition, and create a new Windows Forms Application project. Name the application Weather Tracker.

2. In Solution Explorer, rename Form1.vb to Main.vb.

3. Using the Properties window, change the properties for the Main form using the values in Table 9-1.

Property	Value
Size:Width	660
Size:Height	350
BackColor	System:HotTrack

Table 9-1
Properties for Main.vb

Property	Value
ForeColor	Web:White
Font	Segoe UI 8 Bold
Icon	Sun.ico
MinimizeBox	False
MaximizeBox	False
StartPosition	CenterScreen
FormBorderStyle	FixedDialog
ShowInTaskBar	False
DoubleBuffered	True
WindowState	Minimized

Table 9-1
Properties for Main.vb

MORE INFO

DoubleBuffered helps reduce or prevent flickering when the form is redrawn. The form control is using a secondary buffer to update the form's graphics data, whereby a quick write to the displayed surface memory is then performed, reducing the chances of flickering. If *DoubleBuffered* is not enabled, then progressive redrawing of parts of the displayed form occurs, creating the flickering.

Adding Notification Area Capabilities

Now that you have established the Main form, you'll add the notification area capabilities. Let's talk about terminology. If an application uses an icon located in the notification area (the area on the Windows taskbar where the clock ordinarily appears), this icon is called a *notify icon* and is implemented with a NotifyIcon control. The icon can have a context menu with different actions. Your icon will have a context menu with the following choices: About, Refresh Weather Info, Options, Open, and Exit.

NOTE

The NotifyIcon control does not have a design representation on the form surface, so you'll add it to the component tray at the same place where you added the ADO.NET components in the previous chapter.

TO CREATE A NOTIFYICON CONTROL

1. In the Toolbox, drag a NotifyIcon control from the Common Controls group to the form. It appears in the component tray. Name the control *notifyWeather*.

2. Change its *Text* property to *Weather Tracker*.

3. In the Toolbox, drag a ContextMenuStrip control from the Menus & Toolbars group to the form, and name it *cmsNotify*.

4. Using the Smart Tag on the *cmsNotify* control in the component tray, select Edit Items.... The Items Collection Editor appears.

5. In the Items Collection Editor, change the *cmsNotify* control's properties using the values in Table 9-2.

Property	Value
BackColor	System:Gradient InactiveCaption
ShowImageMargin	False

Table 9-2
Properties for the cmsNotify Control

6. From the Select Item and Add to List Below drop-down list on the left, select MenuItem, and then click the Add button. Change the control's properties using the values shown in Table 9-3.

Property	Value
(Name)	tsmiAbout
Text	About...
ForeColor	System:HotTrack

Table 9-3
Properties for the About Menu Item

7. From the Select Item and Add to List Below drop-down list, select Separator, and click the Add button. Change its *ForeColor* property to *System:HotTrack*.

8. From the Select Item and Add to List Below drop-down list, select MenuItem, and click the Add button. Change the control's properties using the values shown in Table 9-4.

Property	Value
(Name)	tsmiRefresh
Text	Refresh Weather Info
ForeColor	System:HotTrack

Table 9-4
Properties for the Refresh Menu Item

9. From the Select Item and Add to List Below drop-down list, select Separator, and click the Add button. Change its *ForeColor* property to *System:HotTrack*.

10. From the Select Item and Add to List Below drop-down list, select MenuItem, and click the Add button. Change the control's properties using the values shown in Table 9-5.

Property	Value
(Name)	tsmiOptions
Text	Options...
ForeColor	System:HotTrack

Table 9-5
Properties for the Options Menu Item

11. From the Select Item and Add to List Below drop-down list, select Separator, and click the Add button. Change its *ForeColor* property to *System:HotTrack*.

12. From the Select Item and Add to List Below drop-down list, select MenuItem, and click the Add button. Change the control's properties using the values shown in Table 9-6.

Property	Value
(Name)	tsmiOpen
Text	Open...
ForeColor	System:HotTrack

Table 9-6
Properties for the Open Menu Item

13. From the Select Item and Add to List Below drop-down list, select MenuItem, and click the Add button. Change the control's properties using the values shown in Table 9-7.

Property	Value
(Name)	tsmiExit
Text	Exit
ForeColor	System:HotTrack

Table 9-7
Properties for the Exit Menu Item

You're finished adding items to the context menu strip. The Items Collection Editor should look like Figure 9-2.

14. Click OK to close the Items Collection Editor.

You now need to associate the context menu strip with the *notifyWeather* control, which is fairly easy to do.

Figure 9-2
Items for the context menu

TO ASSOCIATE THE CONTEXT MENU STRIP WITH THE CONTROL

1. Select the *notifyWeather* control in the component tray, and in the Properties window, change the *ContextMenuStrip* property to *cmsNotify*.

   You are currently acting as the user. For you to be able to click the application when it's in the notification area, your *notifyWeather* control needs an icon. The icon will later become dynamically generated by your application, and the icon will become the current temperature. Therefore, you now need to associate a temporary icon with the application; otherwise, you will not be able to select it in the notification area.

2. In the Properties window for *notifyWeather*, set the *Icon* property to *otheroptions.ico*. This file is located in a folder named Images in the Chapter9 folder where you installed the companion content.

3. Press F5 to execute the application.

You should see this icon in your notification area:

If you right-click this icon, you should see the context menu shown in Figure 9-3.

Figure 9-3
Context menu of the notifyWeather *control*

When you are finished, the only way to stop the application is to click the blue Stop Debugging button in the Visual Studio toolbar. You will now add another way to stop the application.

TO STOP AN APPLICATION

1. Select the *tsmiExit* control from the Properties window drop-down list.

2. Click the Events button (the yellow lightning icon) in the Properties window, and then double-click the *Click* event to open Code view.

3. Edit the *tsmiExit_Click* event handler, and add the *Shutdown* method as shown in the following code. You're adding the *Shutdown* method because you always want to make your code reusable, and a *Shutdown* method will enable you to do this.

```
1   Private Sub tsmiExit_Click(ByVal sender As System.Object, ByVal e As _
        System.EventArgs) Handles tsmiExit.Click
2       Me.Shutdown()
3   End Sub
4
5   Private Sub Shutdown()
6       If notifyWeather.Visible Then
7           notifyWeather.Visible = False
```

```
8        End If
9        Application.Exit()
10   End Sub
```

The first instruction of the *Shutdown* method will verify whether the *notifyWeather* control is visible and, if it is, will make the notify icon disappear from the notification area. The last line will terminate the application. You will now be able to click the Exit menu item in the context menu to terminate the application; you won't need to use the Stop Debugging button. You can try your application by pressing F5 and then verifying whether the Exit menu item works as expected.

Now you can exit from your application, but you don't have a way to open the Main form, which will have the weather information. To do this, you will want to link the double-click event of the *notifyWeather* control icon in the notification area to the action of opening the Main form in the middle of the screen.

4. In Design view, select the *notifyWeather* control in the component tray. In the events list of the Properties window, double-click the *MouseDoubleClick* event. Edit the *notify-Weather_MouseDoubleClick* event handler, and add the *Restore* method as shown in the following code:

```
11   Private Sub Restore()
12       If Me.WindowState = FormWindowState.Minimized Then
13           Me.WindowState = FormWindowState.Normal
14       End If
15       Me.Visible = True
16   End Sub
17   Private Sub notifyWeather_MouseDoubleClick(ByVal sender As _
         System.Object, ByVal e As System.Windows.Forms.MouseEventArgs) _
         Handles notifyWeather.MouseDoubleClick
18       Me.Restore()
19   End Sub
```

Again, you created a private method called *Restore* in case you need it elsewhere in your application.

The first line of code in the *Restore* method is there because it is impossible to know in which context your method will be called. In your case, when you created the form, you set the *WindowState* property to *minimized* and *ShowInTaskbar* to *false* so that the form starts minimized and the user doesn't see it. When you start the application, the first time the user clicks the Open... menu choice (you'll code this soon) or double-clicks the *notifyWeather* control, the user won't be able to see the form if you have set only its *Visible* property to *true*. Therefore, you need to verify in which window state the form appears. If it's still minimized, you need to set it to *Normal* so that the focus is on the Main form.

5. Press F5 to test the changes. Double-click the *notifyWeather* icon in the notification area, and the Main form should appear.

   Now let's see what happens if the user clicks the Close button (the red X). If you close the application by clicking the Close button, it closes permanently. Yet, our design requirements state that the application should simply minimize to the notification area when the user clicks the Close button. Therefore, you'll now intercept an event that occurs just before the form is closed and just before the form object is deleted, which is an event called *FormClosing*. By using a *FormClosing* event, you can extract the reason for the form's closing and in this way intercept the event when the user clicks the Close button.

6. In Design view, select the Main form. Go to the events list in the Properties window, and double-click the *FormClosing* event. Add the following code to the *Main_FormClosing* event handler:

```
20   Private Sub Main_FormClosing(ByVal sender As System.Object, ByVal e As _
          System.Windows.Forms.FormClosingEventArgs) Handles _
          MyBase.FormClosing
21       If (e.CloseReason = CloseReason.UserClosing) Then
22           e.Cancel = True
23           Me.Hide()
24       End If
25   End Sub
```

MORE INFO

If you want to learn more about why a form is closing, you can search the Help system for *CloseReason* enumeration.

MORE INFO

The *UserClosing* event will also be called whenever the user presses Alt+F4 or whenever the user clicks Close in the form control menu (the menu that appears when you click the left corner where the icon is usually located).

Part of the event is *FormClosingEventArgs*, which contains the arguments that accompany the event notification as well as the reason why the form is closing.

If the user is closing the form, setting the *Cancel* property to *true* will stop the closing process and prevent the form from closing. The next instruction is a call to the *Hide* method. The *Hide* method is simply a synonym for setting the *Visible* property to *false*. The form will simply be hidden.

When the user clicks the Exit item in the context menu, the *FormClosing* event will be raised; however, the reason given will not be *UserClosing*. Instead, it will be *Application-ExitCall*, and therefore the application will continue the closing process.

7. You'll now add the code for the Open... menu choice. To write the code for this event, click *cmsNotify* in the component tray, and then double-click the Open... menu choice on the content menu strip. The *Click* event handler will be created, and you'll call the *Restore* method to handle the form's visibility, which is done by the *Me.Restore()* code. You will write code to make sure the form has the focus so that it ends up on top of any other windows that are displayed. Add the following code to the *tsmiOpen_Click* event handler:

```
26   Private Sub tsmiOpen_Click(ByVal sender As System.Object, ByVal e As _
         System.EventArgs) Handles tsmiOpen.Click
27      Me.Restore()
28      Me.Focus()
29   End Sub
```

Now, test the application with the following test scenario.

Start the application by pressing F5. Right-click the notify icon, and select Open.... The Main form should appear in the middle of your screen. Minimize the Main form by clicking the Close button. Once it is minimized, double-click the notify icon. You should see the Main form again. Terminate the application by click the Exit menu item.

Adding the Splash Screen and About Dialog Box

Since you created a splash screen and an About dialog box in Chapter 6, "Modifying Your Web Browser," I won't spend too much time on those topics in this section. You merely need to add two new forms to your project and name them SplashWeatherTracker.vb and AboutWeatherTracker.vb. Don't forget to use the correct template when you add the form to the project; if you don't, you won't be able to access all of the prepopulated information.

Using the values in Table 9-8, set the specified properties for the SplashWeather form. The location of your labels doesn't matter; place them wherever you want. Any images are located in the Images folder under Chapter9 where you installed the companion content.

Component	Property	Value
SplashWeatherTracker	StartPosition	CenterScreen
MainLayoutPanel	BackgroundImage	Mountain.jpg
Main LayoutPanel	BackgroundImageLayout	Stretch
ApplicationTitle	Font	Segoe UI 20 Regular
ApplicationTitle	ForeColor	Web:White
Version	Font	Segoe UI 9 Bold
Version	ForeColor	Web:White
Copyright	Font	Segoe UI 9 Bold
Copyright	ForeColor	Web:White

Table 9-8
Properties for SplashWeather.vb

Using the values in Table 9-9, set the specified properties on the AboutWeatherTracker form.

Component	Property	Value
AboutWeatherTracker	Font	Segoe UI 8 Regular
AboutWeatherTracker	BackColor	System:HotTrack
AboutWeatherTracker	StartPosition	CenterScreen
AboutWeatherTracker	ForeColor	Web:White
TextBoxDescription	Font	Segoe UI 8 Regular

Table 9-9
Properties for AboutWeatherTracker.vb

Component	Property	Value
TextBoxDescription	BackColor	System:HotTrack
TextBoxDescription	ForeColor	Web:White
OKButton	FlatStyle	Flat
LogoPictureBox	Image	Sunset.jpg

Table 9-9 (continued)
Properties for AboutWeatherTracker.vb

Now you need to attach these two forms to the rest of the application.

TO ATTACH FORMS TO AN APPLICATION

1. To attach the splash screen, you'll use the Project Designer. In Solution Explorer, right-click the Weather Tracker project, and select Properties. On the Application tab, set the Splash Screen drop-down list to SplashWeatherTracker.

2. While you are at it, you'll change the application icon to Sun.ico. In the Icon drop-down list, select <Browse...>. Select the Sun.ico file in the Chapter9 Images folder.

3. Click Assembly Information, and set the assembly information for the project. This information will fill the splash screen and About dialog box fields.

4. To attach the About box, you need to tie it to the context About... menu item. Go to your Main.vb form in design mode.

5. Select *cmsNotify* in the component tray, and double-click the About... menu choice in the context menu strip. Add the following code to the *tsmiAbout_Click* event handler:

```
1  Private Sub tsmiAbout_Click(ByVal sender As System.Object, ByVal e As _
       System.EventArgs) Handles tsmiAbout.Click
2      AboutWeatherTracker.ShowDialog()
3  End Sub
```

Adding the Options Dialog Box

You now have three forms. You will add the final Options dialog box form that will appear when the user clicks the Options... menu item in the context menu after clicking the notify icon.

TO ADD THE OPTIONS DIALOG BOX FORM

NOTE

At this point in the chapter, the current project state is saved in the Chapter9 companion content in a folder named Weather Tracker UI. To add the Web service functionality, you can continue with your own project or use the project in Weather Tracker UI.

1. In Solution Explorer, right-click Weather Tracker, select Add, and then click Windows Form in the context menu.

2. From the templates, select Windows Form, name the form Options.vb, and then click Add.

3. Using the values in Table 9-10, set properties and add controls to the Options form so that it looks like the form shown in Figure 9-4.

Figure 9-4
The Options form

Component	Control Type	Property	Value
Options	Form	Font	Segoe UI 8 Regular
Options	Form	BackColor	System:HotTrack
Options	Form	StartPosition	CenterScreen
Options	Form	ForeColor	Web:White
Options	Form	ControlBox	False
Options	Form	FormBorderStyle	FixedDialog
Option	Form	MaximizeBox	False
Options	Form	MinimizeBox	False

Table 9-10
Properties and Controls for the Options Dialog Box

Component	Control Type	Property	Value
Options	Form	Text	Options
Options	Form	Size:Width	295
Options	Form	Size:Height	295
txtCurrentCity	Textbox	AcceptReturn	True
txtCurrentCity	Textbox	BackColor	System:InactiveCaption
lblCurrentCity	Label	Text	Current City:
lbPossibleCities	ListBox	BackColor	System:InactiveCaption
lbPossibleCities	ListBox	Cursor	Hand
lbPossibleCities	ListBox	SelectionMode	One
lbPossibleCities	ListBox	ForeColor	Web:White
btnOk	Button	BackColor	System:InactiveCaption
btnOk	Button	FlatStyle	Popup
btnOk	Button	Text	Ok
btnCancel	Button	BackColor	System:InactiveCaption
btnCancel	Button	Text	Cancel
btnCancel	Button	FlatStyle	Popup
Options	Form	CancelButton	btnCancel
rbCelsius	Radio Button	BackColor	System:HotTrack
rbFahrenheit	RadioButton	BackColor	System:HotTrack
rbFahrenheit	RadioButton	Checked	True
lblUnit	Label	Text	Unit

Table 9-10
Properties and Controls for the Options Dialog Box

TO HOOK UP THE FORM TO THE CONTEXT MENU

1. Display the Main form in design mode.

2. Click *cmsNotify* in the component tray, and double-click the Options... menu item in the context menu strip.

3. At the top of Main.vb, just below *Public Class Main*, add the following line of code:

```
Dim optionsForm as New Options()
```

4. Add the following lines of code to the *tsiOptions_Click* event handler:

```
1  Private Sub tsmiOptions_Click(ByVal sender As System.Object, ByVal e _
       As System.EventArgs) Handles tsmiOptions.Click
2      optionsForm.ShowDialog()
3  End Sub
```

5. Press F5 to run the application. You should see your splash screen. Use the context menu on the notify icon to open the About dialog box and the Options dialog box. When you have finished, exit the application.

You are now finished with this part of the project. Be sure to save your project. It is time to get to the meat of the project: using the MSN Weather service.

Using the MSN Weather Web Service

You have constructed a nice shell, but the shell is rather empty at this moment. You need to access weather data in order to populate the shell. To accomplish this, you will learn to consume Web services. But first, what is a Web service?

A *Web service* is an application that runs on a Web server such as Internet Information Services (IIS). A Web service has a series of exposed public methods that an application can call. You'll find numerous examples of Web services on the Internet. You can use Web services that perform a variety of operations, such as finding a ZIP code, viewing a map, buying movie tickets, looking for information on search engines such as MSN or Google, and accessing weather information like your application will soon do. In the .NET world, classes and wizards are available to help you consume Web services. There are two popular implementations of Web services in use on the Web: SOAP and REST.

SOAP Web services use XML to send messages and return results. All objects are serialized (the messages are sent as a series of bits and pieces over the Internet) and are then deserialized on the other side into objects. The beauty of XML Web services is that they can be hosted and consumed on any operating system and developed in any language. Because they use a series of standardized protocols and rules, XML Web services promote interoperability and efficiency. The future of the transacted world over the Internet lies in big part with the success of Web services.

REST Web services use HTTP to make calls to services and receive XML data. They are lighter to use and implement, and you call them just as you would type a URL in a browser. For instance, *http://www.foobar.com/parts/111* will call a Web service and get you the details about a part with the part number 111. The XML coming back to your browser would be the details of that part. REST stands for Representational State Transfer. It's not a standard like SOAP is; it is simply an architectural style. However, although it's not a standard, it does prescribe the use of many standards such as XML, HTTP, URL, HTML, and so on.

In this project, you will use REST Web services as offered by MSN.

IMPORTANT

You will need to be connected to the Internet to follow the steps in the rest of the chapter; otherwise, nothing will work from this point on, especially in the next section because that's where you're communicating with the Web service.

Trying a Web Service

You can use your regular Web browser to try a SOAP or REST Web service without writing a line of code. You can usually point your Web browser to the Web service address and invoke its methods. This is an excellent way to learn what a Web method needs and what its output looks like. (Please note that it's not possible to talk to all of them in this way.) As an example, try a SOAP Web service that returns a currency conversion rate between two currencies: http://www.webservicex.com/CurrencyConvertor.asmx. *Click the* ConversionRate *method, scroll down until you see two text boxes, type* **CAD** *and* **USD** *in the two text boxes, and then click Invoke. In a separate browser, you will obtain XML and the conversion rate (as of today).*

To test a REST Web service, you can use the same URL that you will use in code later in this chapter. In your browser, type the following: http://weather.service.msn.com/data.aspx?src=vista&wealocations=wc:USWA0367. *In the same browser tab or window, you'll see the XML representing weather information for the city of Redmond, Washington.*

NOTE

In Chapter 8, "Managing the Data," you learned that you could create data sources from a Web service, a database, or an object. In this section, that's exactly what you'll benefit from here. You will see how reusing tools and components allows you to be more productive. You will use the same techniques used in the previous database examples, except that this time you will be binding data coming across the wire from all parts of the globe.

Connecting to MSN Weather Web Services

You will now build a business logic DLL to get the data and then display the object returned by the different methods in that DLL.

First you will create a .NET assembly that will contain the information used to communicate with MSN and also to map to items in the user interface you'll define later.

TO CONNECT TO A WEB SERVICE

1. Click File, Add, New Project, and then select the Class Library template. Type **Weather-Report** for the class library name.

2. In your class library, rename class1.vb to WeatherReport.vb.

3. Add a reference to the *System.Drawing* namespace, and while you're in Solution Explorer, add a reference to your newly created class library to your WeatherTracker project.

4. To use the bitmap, you'll have to add an *Imports* statement to your code. To do this, open the WeatherReport.vb file, and add the following:

```
Imports System.Drawing
```

5. This time, instead of binding the data to a database as you did in Chapter 8, you'll bind the Web service data to an object that will then be bound to items on your form. Now add the fields and properties in Table 9-11 to your WeatherReport.vb file. To add a field and a property quickly and correctly, you will use a snippet. Open the WeatherReport.vb file, and then for each field listed in the table, right-click in the editor, and select Insert Snippet/Code Patterns—If, For Each, Try Catch, Property, etc/Properties, Procedures, Events/Define a Property.

Field	Property	Type
currentTemperatureValue	CurrentTemperature	Integer
feelsLikeTemperatureValue	FeelsLikeTemperature	Integer

Table 9-11
Fields and Properties for WeatherReport.vb

Microsoft Visual Basic 2008 Express Edition: Build a Program Now!

Field	Property	Type
humidityValue	Humidity	Integer
lastUpdateValue	LastUpdate	DateTime
locationValue	Location	String
minTemperatureForecastValue	MinTemperatureForecast	Integer
maxTemperatureForecastValue	MaxTemperatureForecast	Integer
skyCodeValue	SkyCode	Integer
skyTextValue	SkyText	String
skyImageValue	SkyImage	Bitmap
locationCodeValue	LocationCode	String

Table 9-11
Fields and Properties for WeatherReport.vb

6. Save your file after adding all the fields and properties.

7. Build your solution by pressing Ctrl+Shift+B.

Now you'll add the weather information to your form.

TO ADD WEATHER INFORMATION TO YOUR FORM

1. Make sure you are viewing the Main form on the designer surface.

2. Go to the Data Sources window, and then select Add New Data Source....

3. You will see the familiar Data Source Configuration Wizard, but this time select Object instead of Database.

4. You'll add a reference to your newly created class library since this object will be the one you'll use to map the data from the Web service and the data displayed on your form. Click the Add Reference... button, and on the Projects tab select your WeatherReport

class library. Your screen should display the wizard with the WeatherReport assembly added, as shown in Figure 9-5. Click Next to continue and then the Finish button.

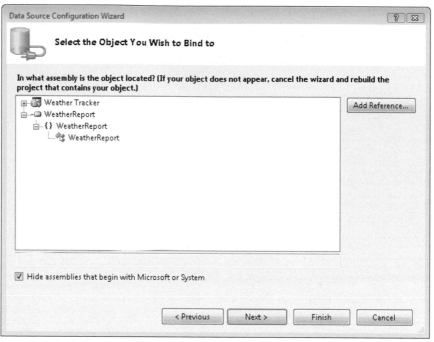

Figure 9-5
Data Source Configuration Wizard with the WeatherReport assembly selected

Figure 9-6
Data Sources tab with the newly created WeatherReport data source

You should see the WeatherReport data source on the Data Sources tab beside Solution Explorer. Refer to Figure 9-6 to make sure you're at the right place.

5. As you can see in Figure 9-6, the data source name is actually also a drop-down control. Click it, and select Details. Then click the plus sign to expand it and see the details of your data source that was created from your WeatherReport class library assembly. You'll see that all the properties you created are represented in the data source.

6. Expand the WeatherReport node, and change all the element types (except SkyImage) from TextBox to Label by clicking the down arrow on each element and selecting Label from the drop-down list.

7. Drag WeatherReport to the Main form design surface. This creates all the fields and labels for you. The design might not be what you want, but at least it's partially done for you. You'll fix this in a minute. Note that two new controls have been added to the component tray: WeatherReportBindingSource and WeatherReportBindingNavigator.

8. Click WeatherReportBindingNavigator in the component tray, and change its *Visible* property to *false*. (You might need to click the Properties button at the top of the Properties window to see the list of properties.)

9. You can't see the boundaries of all the controls on the form. To help with layout, select all the controls on the form by creating a large selection rectangle around them with your mouse pointer. In the Properties window, change *BorderStyle* from *None* to *FixedSingle*. Black borders should appear around all controls. Once the form is done, you'll reset *BorderStyle* to *None*.

10. Now you can start modifying the layout and look and feel of your form. For the PictureBox control, set the *Name* property to *pbSkyImage*, set the *BackColor* property to *Web:White*, set the *Size.Width* property to *55*, and set the *Size.Height* property to *45*.

11. Delete the Sky Image: label.

12. Add a Label control, and set the *Text* property to *Current Weather*.

13. Add a Label control, and set the *Text* property to *Contacting MSN Weather Service* and the *Visible* property to *False*.

14. Add a PictureBox control, and set *Visible* to *False* and *Image* to *progressbar_green.gif* from the Images folder.

15. Using Figure 9-7 as a guide, size and position the controls on the form. If you want, adjust the font size and style of the labels.

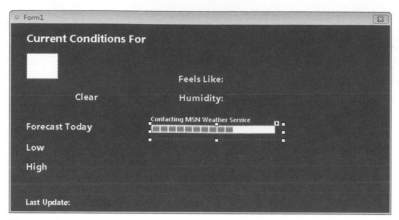

Figure 9-7
Layout of the current weather information

Setting User and Application Preferences

The application settings are stored in an XML file and persist from one execution to another. The current location code will be saved here so that a user doesn't have to re-enter the location every time your application starts.

TO CREATE USER SETTING ENTRIES

1. In Solution Explorer, right-click the Weather Tracker project, and select Properties. The Project Designer appears.

2. On the Settings tab, add entries for CurrentLocationCode and CurrentUnit, as shown in Figure 9-8.

Name	Type	Scope	Value
CurrentLocatio...	String	User	wc:USWA0367
CurrentUnit	String	User	F
CurrentLocation	String	User	Redmond, Washington

Figure 9-8
Application settings in the Project Designer

All entries are strongly typed (that is, a real .NET type) and set to type *String*. The scope field is set to User, which means this setting is related to user preferences and the user can change it during execution. This type of setting will be persisted from one execution to another. The other possible setting is Application-scoped, which is usually associated with an application that uses a database connection string. Users can't change those settings at execution time.

3. Save your project, and close the Project Designer.

Working in the Background

If you try to run your form now, you won't get anything from the Web service; you'll get only the default text you might have entered. This process differs from your work with databases, in which a great deal of code was completed for you so you could retrieve the data and populate the fields. When dealing with a Web service, you must do more of the actual coding to get the data into the form. Let's talk about how you'll do this.

Talking to a Web service can be a long process. This typically means only a few seconds (perhaps up to 30 seconds), but you can't leave the user with a blocked UI while your application is retrieving information. You therefore need a way of saying to your application: "Go get this information, and let me know when you have it." This programming technique is called *multithreaded programming with callbacks*. Since .NET Framework 2.0, this type of programming is simplified by a new class called *BackgroundWorker*. As its name implies, it works in the background on a task; what's not implied is that it will let you know when it has completed the task.

TO ADD THE MSN WEATHER DATA CLASS

To communicate and retrieve the data from the MSN Weather service, you'll create a new class called MSNWeatherData.vb and add it to your project. This class will insulate you from the service and its technicalities; it's an OOP technique called *abstraction*, which enables you (or somebody else using your class) to just say, "Give me the weather report for a location. I know it returns a *WeatherReport* object, and that's all I need in order to integrate the weather report into my application." In addition, you can use the *MSNWeatherData* class in other applications. Isn't that cool?

To talk to the MSN Weather service and return the data from the *WeatherReport* class, you've already created a DLL to handle the mapping between the form and the code; you also enabled the data binding on an object. In the following code, you'll see that to connect to the MSN Web service and read the data, you have to use a simple *XMLTextReader* to connect to the server and open the resulting XML. Here are the two methods in this class; the code is not really difficult to understand because it is repetitive, but essentially it's just a task of mapping the correct XML file and mapping the methods to the appropriate fields in the *WeatherReport* class.

1. Add the following code to the *WeatherReport* class.

```
Function GetWeatherReport(ByVal LocationCode As String) As _
    WeatherReport.WeatherReport
    ' create a WeatherReport instance so that we can load the data from
    ' the Web service call and then map it to the UI.
    Dim currentWeatherReport As New WeatherReport.WeatherReport()

    ' URL corresponding to the MSN REST Web Service - see how the
    ' locationCode is passed in a parameter to this URL.
    ' The XMLTextReader opens up the URL and receives the XML returned
    ' by the server
    Dim feedUrl = _
    http://weather.service.msn.com/data.aspx?src=vista&wealocations=  _
        & LocationCode
    Dim reader As New XmlTextReader(feedUrl)
    Dim firstForecastDone As Boolean = False
    Dim skyImagesRelativeUrl As String = "images/"

    Try
        ' The rest is just extraction and mapping of the meaningful
        ' data points.
        While (reader.Read ())
            If ((reader.NodeType = XmlNodeType.Element) And _
                (reader.Name = "weather")) Then
                reader.MoveToAttribute("weatherlocationname")
                currentWeatherReport.Location = reader.Value
            ElseIf ((reader.NodeType = XmlNodeType.Element) And _
```

```
        ((reader.Name = "forecast") _
            And (firstForecastDone = False))) Then
        firstForecastDone = True
        reader.MoveToAttribute("high")
        Integer.TryParse(reader.Value, _
            currentWeatherReport.MaxTemperatureForecast)

        reader.MoveToAttribute("low")
        Integer.TryParse(reader.Value, _
            currentWeatherReport.MinTemperatureForecast)
    ElseIf ((reader.NodeType = XmlNodeType.Element) And _
        (reader.Name = "current")) Then
        reader.MoveToAttribute("temperature")
        Integer.TryParse(reader.Value, _
            currentWeatherReport.CurrentTemperature)

        reader.MoveToAttribute("feelslike")
        Integer.TryParse(reader.Value, _
            currentWeatherReport.FeelsLikeTemperature)

        reader.MoveToAttribute("humidity")
        Integer.TryParse(reader.Value, _
            currentWeatherReport.Humidity)

        reader.MoveToAttribute("skytext")
        currentWeatherReport.SkyText = reader.Value

        reader.MoveToAttribute("skycode")
        Integer.TryParse(reader.Value, _
            currentWeatherReport.SkyCode)
        Dim fileName As String = skyImagesRelativeUrl & _
            currentWeatherReport.SkyCode & ".tif"
        currentWeatherReport.SkyImage = New Bitmap(fileName)

        reader.MoveToAttribute("observationtime")
        Dim splitter As Char() = ":"
        Dim hourMinuteSecond As String() = _
            reader.Value.Split(splitter)
        Dim hour, minute, second As Integer
        Integer.TryParse(hourMinuteSecond(0), hour)
        Integer.TryParse(hourMinuteSecond(1), minute)
        Integer.TryParse(hourMinuteSecond(2), second)
```

```
                            reader.MoveToAttribute("date")
                            splitter = "-"
                            Dim yearMonthDay As String() = _
                                reader.Value.Split(splitter)
                            Dim year, month, day As Integer
                            Integer.TryParse(yearMonthDay(0), year)
                            Integer.TryParse(yearMonthDay(1), month)
                            Integer.TryParse(yearMonthDay(2), day)
                            currentWeatherReport.LastUpdate = New DateTime(year, _
                                month, day, hour, minute, second)
                    End If
                End While
                ' We return a valid weather report.
                Return currentWeatherReport
            Catch ex As Exception
                Throw ex
            End Try
        End Function


        Function GetLocations(ByVal Query As String) As _
            List(Of KeyValuePair(Of String, String))
            If ((Query = "") Or (Query.Length < 2)) Then
                Return Nothing
            Else
                ' Because the ListBox in the Options UI can't bind with a
                ' generic collection that doesn't support IList or IListSource;
                ' that's why you use a generic List(Of Items you really need)
                ' you are able to load
                Dim results As New List(Of KeyValuePair(Of String, String))
                Dim searchUrl As String = _
"http://weather.service.msn.com/find.aspx?outputview=search&src=vista&wease
archstr=" & Query
                Dim reader As New XmlTextReader(searchUrl)
                Dim locationCode As String
                Dim locationFullName As String

                While (reader.Read())
                    If ((reader.NodeType = XmlNodeType.Element) And _
                        (reader.Name = "weather")) Then
                        reader.MoveToAttribute("weatherfullname")
```

```
            locationFullName = reader.Value
            reader.MoveToAttribute("weatherlocationcode")
            locationCode = reader.Value
            Dim pair As KeyValuePair(Of String, String) = _
                New KeyValuePair(Of String, String)(locationCode, _
                locationFullName)
            results.Add(pair)
        End If
    End While
    Return results
End If
End Function
```

Now that you've created the two methods required to obtain information from the MSN REST Weather service, you'll add the code to do it asynchronously.

TO PERFORM A TASK IN THE BACKGROUND

1. Open the Main form in Design view.

2. Go to the Toolbox. In the Components section, select the BackgroundWorker control, and drag it to your form. It doesn't have a design-time portion, so it will be added to the component tray. Rename it *BackgroundCurrentWorker*.

3. At the top of the Properties window for *BackgroundCurrentWorker*, click the Events button (the yellow lightning icon), and then double-click the *DoWork* event.

4. Add the following code to the *BackgroundCurrentWorker_DoWork* event handler:

```
Private Sub BackgroundCurrentWorker_DoWork(ByVal sender As System.Object, _
    ByVal e As System.ComponentModel.DoWorkEventArgs) Handles _
    BackgroundCurrentWorker.DoWork
    ' This method will execute in the background thread created
    ' by the BackgroundWorker component
    Dim desiredLocationCode As String = e.Argument
    Dim myMSNWeather As New MSNWeatherData()
    e.Result = myMSNWeather.GetWeatherReport(desiredLocationCode)

End Sub
```

The *DoWork* event handler is where the call to the MSN Weather service takes place. You will start by calling the *GetWeatherReport* method. When you invoke the *GetWeather-Report* method, it runs in a separate context so that it doesn't block the application UI. Otherwise, the application could appear to be in a "frozen" state. The *GetWeatherReport* method takes one parameter and returns a *WeatherReport* result.

5. Add the following *startBackgroundGetCurrentWeather* method:

```
Private Sub startBackgroundGetCurrentWeather()
    ' Execute the Background Task only if it's not already working
    If Not (BackgroundCurrentWorker.IsBusy()) Then
        Me.UseWaitCursor = True
        Me.lblProgress.Visible = True
        Me.PictureBoxProgress.Visible = True
        BackgroundCurrentWorker.RunWorkerAsync(currentLocationCode)
    End If

End Sub
```

The *startBackgroundGetCurrentWeather* method starts the *BackgroundWorker* component. You first need to verify whether *BackgroundWorker* is already busy with a previous call; if you don't do this, you'll end up with an *InvalidOperationException*. Simply verifying whether *BackgroundWorker* is busy ensures that you won't get that exception when calling the *RunWorkerAsync* method. In fact, this is the only exception that this method can raise. A quick look at the documentation can confirm this.

Executing the *RunWorkerAsync* method means submitting a request to start an operation asynchronously, which raises the *DoWork* event. An event handler with the following name format is invoked: *<your backgroundworker variable>_DoWork*. In this case, the *BackgroundCurrentWorker_DoWork* method is executed when the *DoWork* event is raised.

6. Switch to Design view, and click *BackgroundCurrentWorker* in the component tray.

7. In the events list in the Properties window, double-click the *RunWorkerCompleted* event.

8. Add the following code to the *BackgroundCurrentWorker_RunWorkerCompleted* event handler:

```
Dim currentWeatherReport As WeatherReport.WeatherReport
    If (e.Error Is Nothing) Then
```

```
        Me.UseWaitCursor = False
        Me.lblProgress.Visible = False
        Me.PictureBoxProgress.Visible = False

        ' This event fires when the DoWork event completes
        currentWeatherReport = e.Result
        If (currentUnit = "C") Then
            Me.ConvertToMetric(currentWeatherReport)
        End If
        WeatherReportBindingSource.DataSource = currentWeatherReport
        ' Refresh the display based on the new data binding and
        ' update the labels with the proper temperature unit.
        WeatherReportBindingSource.ResetBindings(False)
        UpdateUnitLabels()

        ' If Web service returned weather info, then
        ' update notify icon
        Me.CreateIcon(currentWeatherReport.CurrentTemperature)
    Else
        MessageBox.Show( _
        "Problem with the MSN Weather Web service! Error message:" + _
        vbLf + e.Error.Message + vbLf + "Retry Later!", _
        "Weather Web service problem")
End If
```

If the MSN Web service is available, the method you invoked is working in a different context and on its own. When it is finished with its business, you will be notified that the method has completed, because a *RunWorkerCompleted* event will be raised.

To retrieve the results, you must have an event handler with the following name: *<your backgroundworker variable>_RunWorkerCompleted*. In this method, you have a parameter of type *RunWorkerCompletedEventArgs* that contains everything you need to obtain the results. If an exception was raised in the *DoWork* event handler, you'll be able to retrieve it by checking the *Error* property, which is of type *Exception*. If there is no error, you must retrieve the results yourself. Remember that the *Results* property will give you an element of type *Object*, which by itself will not help you. You need to assign it a variable with the same type as the binding class you created (that is, *WeatherReport*) to pass data back and forth between the Web service and the form.

If you recall, when you dragged the *WeatherReport* object to the designer surface, you automatically created data-bound controls for all of those fields. Thus, you simply need to assign that *currentWeatherReport* variable as the data source for *BindingSource*, and you will have a link between what's coming from the Web service and the controls on your form. In addition, you have to make a call to *ResetBindings(False)*, which will enable *BindingSource* to refresh the form and therefore display the new content for that location. After that, the method called simply adds the proper unit to the different temperatures, that is, Celsius or Fahrenheit. What happens next is the creation of the icon that will appear in the notification area representing the current temperature.

TO ADD SUPPORTING BACKGROUND CODE

1. At the very top of Main.vb, add the following *Imports* statements:

```
1   Imports System.Runtime.InteropServices
2   Imports System.Net
```

2. At the top of the class, add the following lines just below *Public Class Main*:

```
Public Shared currentTemperature As Double
Public Shared currentLocationCode As String = My.Settings.CurrentLocationCode
Public Shared currentLocation As String =   My.Settings.CurrentLocation
Public Shared currentUnit As String = My.Settings.CurrentUnit
```

The first line of code is declared as a *Public Shared* field named *currentTemperature*. A shared field simply means the field doesn't belong to any particular instance of that class, but that there is only one for the entire class. The *currentLocationCode*, *currentLocation*, and *currentUnit* fields found in the next lines are also shared fields. They are initialized from the user settings, but they will change once you complete the Options form. They are also used to carry the changes made in the Options form back to the Main form.

3. Add the following *UpdateWeather* method:

```
15   Public Sub UpdateWeather()
16       Try
17           Me.tsmiRefresh.Enabled = False
18           Me.tsmiOptions.Enabled = False
19           Me.startBackgroundGetCurrentWeather()
20           Me.tsmiRefresh.Enabled = True
21           Me.tsmiOptions.Enabled = True
22       Catch webEx As WebException
```

```
23            MessageBox.Show( _
24                "MSN Web service currently unavailable" + vbCrLf + _
25                "Retry later using the Refresh Weather Info menu.", _
26                "Web Exception")
27            Me.tsmiRefresh.Enabled = True
28        Catch ex As Exception
29            MessageBox.Show( _
30                "Unknown problem. Error message:" + vbCrLf _
31                + ex.Message + vbCrLf + _
32                "Please, retry later!", "Unknown error")
33            Me.tsmiRefresh.Enabled = True
34        End Try
35    End Sub
```

The *UpdateWeather* method initiates the update of the weather data by calling the *start-BackgroundGetCurrentWeather* method you added earlier. The weather data needs to be updated when the location is changed or when the Refresh Weather Info menu choice is clicked in the context menu of the notify icon. The *UpdateWeather* method also enables or disables menu choices on the context menu as appropriate.

Completing the Core Weather Tracker Functionality

In the next sections, you will add more code to set up a working version of the Weather Tracker application. This includes creating the icon, verifying connectivity, verifying weather Web service availability, and performing other tasks.

First you will add code to create and destroy the icon in the notification area. You can review the code, but I won't discuss it in much detail because GDI+ and COM "interop" are subjects that are too advanced for this book. However, you can refer to the comments within the code to learn more.

TO ADD THE CREATE AND DESTROY NOTIFICATION ICON CODE

1. In Main.vb, add the following *CreateIcon* method:

```
1   Private Sub CreateIcon(ByVal temperature As Integer)
2       Dim displayString As String
```

```
3          Dim drawnIcon As Bitmap
4          Dim brushToDrawString As SolidBrush
5          Dim iconColor As Color
6          Dim iconGraphic As Graphics
7          Dim fontFamily As New FontFamily("Arial")
8          Dim IconFont As New Font( _
9              fontFamily, _
10             11, _
11             FontStyle.Regular, _
12             GraphicsUnit.Pixel)
13
14
15         If (currentUnit = "F") Then
16             If (temperature = Integer.MinValue) Then
17                 displayString = "NA"
18                 iconColor = Color.Red
19             ElseIf (temperature > 100) Then
20                 iconColor = Color.Red
21                 displayString = (temperature - 100).ToString()
22             ElseIf ((temperature < 32) And (temperature > 0)) Then
23                 iconColor = Color.Violet
24                 displayString = temperature.ToString()
25             ElseIf (temperature < 0) Then
26                 iconColor = Color.Blue
27                 displayString = (temperature * -1).ToString()
28             Else
29                 iconColor = Color.White
30                 displayString = temperature.ToString()
31             End If
32         Else
33             If (temperature = Integer.MinValue) Then
34                 displayString = "NA"
35                 iconColor = Color.Red
36             ElseIf (temperature > 38) Then
37                 iconColor = Color.Red
38                 displayString = (temperature).ToString()
39             ElseIf (temperature < 0) Then
40                 iconColor = Color.Violet
41                 displayString = (temperature * -1).ToString()
42             ElseIf (temperature < -18) Then
43                 iconColor = Color.Blue
44                 displayString = (temperature * -1).ToString()
```

```
45        Else
46            iconColor = Color.White
47            displayString = temperature.ToString()
48        End If
49    End If
50
51    ' Start by creating a new bitmap the size of an icon
52    drawnIcon = New Bitmap(16, 16)
53
54    'To draw the string we need a brush
55    brushToDrawString = New SolidBrush(iconColor)
56
57    ' Creating a new graphic object so that we
58    ' can call the drawstring method with our
59    ' temperature or NA if there is no temp.
60    iconGraphic = Graphics.FromImage(drawnIcon)
61
62    ' Now we are drawing the temperature string onto
63    ' graphic and therefore on the bitmap.
64    iconGraphic.DrawString(displayString, IconFont, _
65        brushToDrawString, 0, 0)
66
67    ' We are getting ready to convert the bitmap into
68    ' an icon and to set the notifyWeather.Icon with
69    ' this newly created icon
70    Dim hIcon As IntPtr = drawnIcon.GetHicon()
71    Dim customMadeIcon As Icon = _
72        Drawing.Icon.FromHandle(hIcon)
73    notifyWeather.Icon = customMadeIcon
74
75    'Now that we're done manipulating the new icon
76    ' we need to destroy the unmanaged resource,
77    ' otherwise we'll have a handle leak.
78    DestroyIcon(hIcon)
79 End Sub
```

2. Add the following *DestroyIcon* method:

```
57 ' The GetIcon method generated an unmanaged handle
58 ' that we need to take care of; otherwise, there
59 ' will be a handle leak.
```

```
60  <DllImport("user32.dll", EntryPoint:="DestroyIcon")> _
61  Public Shared Function DestroyIcon( _
62      ByVal hIcon As IntPtr) As Boolean
63  End Function
```

TO FINISH THE MAIN FORM

1. In Design view, select the Main form. In the Properties window, go to the events list, and double-click the *Load* event.

2. Add the following code to the *Main_Load* event handler:

```
1 Private Sub Main_Load(ByVal sender As Object, ByVal e As _
      System.EventArgs) Handles Me.Load
2      'Changing the title of our main form with the
3      'application name and the version
4      Me.Text = My.Application.Info.Title + " " + _
5          My.Application.Info.Version.ToString()
6
7      'Creating temporarily the NA icon.
8      Me.CreateIcon(Integer.MinValue)
9      tsmiRefresh.Enabled = False
10         Me.UpdateWeather()
11     End If
12 End Sub
```

The *Main_Load* event handler is the starting point for Weather Tracker. In this code, you're using the *My* code construct to build the title of the application by using its name and the version stored in the assembly parameters in the same manner that the About box uses this information. Next, a red NA (not available) icon is drawn in the notification area and remains there until the Web service returns with positive results, in which case the temperature will be drawn as an icon. If everything is working as expected, the process for obtaining the weather data starts.

3. In Design view, click *cmsNotify* in the component tray. In the context menu strip, double-click the Refresh Weather Info menu item.

4. Add the following code to the *tsmiRefresh_Click* event handler. This code initiates an update of the weather data when the Refresh Weather Info menu item in the context menu is clicked.

```
33  Private Sub tsmiRefresh_Click(ByVal sender As System.Object, _
       ByVal e As System.EventArgs) Handles tsmiRefresh.Click
34     Me.tsmiRefresh.Enabled = False
35     Me.UpdateWeather()
36  End Sub
```

5. In Design view, select all the controls on the Main form. Set the *BorderStyle* property to *None*. (You might need to click the Properties button at the top of the Properties window to see the list of properties.)

You need to copy all of the weather forecast images from your companion content folder to the same folder where the Weather Tracker application is located. Specifically, you need to create a folder called Images and copy all of the *.tif weather image files into this folder. You'll do this next.

Weather Links

You may be wondering what the link is between the index and the filename and who is creating that link. This is a convention used by many weather providers on the Internet; therefore, this is something that will work with many services if you want to add some later.

TO ADD WEATHER ICONS

1. In Solution Explorer, right-click the Weather Tracker project, select Add, and then select New Folder. Name the folder Images.

2. Using Windows Explorer, copy the *.tif images (1.tif through 47.tif) from the companion content to the Images folder you just created. (The default location for the companion content is Documents\Microsoft Press\VB 2008 Express\Chapter9\Images.)

3. In Solution Explorer, right-click the Images folder, select Add, and then select Existing Item. The Add Existing Item dialog box appears.

4. In the Files of Type drop-down list, select Image Files.

5. Make sure you are looking in the Images folder, and select all the .tif files. To select all the files, you can press Ctrl+A, or you can use Shift-click.

Figure 9-9
Weather icons added to the project

6. When all the .tif files have been selected, click the Add button to add the images to the Weather Tracker project.

7. In Solution Explorer, select all the .tif files. First, select 1.tif, and then, while pressing the Shift key, select the last .tif file.

8. With all the .tif files selected, in the Properties window, set the *Copy to Output Directory* property to *Copy Always*, as shown in Figure 9-9. Make sure the *Build Action* property is set to *Content*.

TO ADD UNIT LABELS AND A CONVERSION UTILITY

The data that comes back from the MSN Weather service is always in Fahrenheit, and if the user wants to have the information in Celsius, you'll need to provide a small tool to do that. The main form doesn't contain any indication about whether the data points are in Fahrenheit or Celsius, which is why you need a conversion tool to give the application time to add the degree symbol and the unit.

1. Add the following code to Main.vb to do both:

```
Public Sub ConvertToMetric(ByRef report As WeatherReport.WeatherReport) _
    report.CurrentTemperature = 5 / 9 * (report.CurrentTemperature - 32)
    report.FeelsLikeTemperature = 5 / 9 * (report.FeelsLikeTemperature - 32)
    report.MaxTemperatureForecast = 5 / 9 *(report.MaxTemperatureForecast - 32)
    report.MinTemperatureForecast = 5 / 9 *(report.MinTemperatureForecast - 32)
End Sub

Public Sub UpdateUnitLabels()
    CurrentTemperatureLabel1.Text = _
        CurrentTemperatureLabel1.Text & "°" & currentUnit
    FeelsLikeTemperatureLabel1.Text = _
        FeelsLikeTemperatureLabel1.Text & "°" & currentUnit
    MinTemperatureForecastLabel1.Text = _
        MinTemperatureForecastLabel1.Text & "°" & currentUnit
    MaxTemperatureForecastLabel1.Text = _
        MaxTemperatureForecastLabel1.Text & "°" & currentUnit
    HumidityLabel1.Text = HumidityLabel1.Text & "%"
End Sub
```

Testing Weather Tracker

Now you will see whether your application works. Press F5 to run Weather Tracker. If you have any build errors, review the errors on the Error List tab, and fix them. If necessary, you can review the completed application in the Complete folder. When you run the application, you should see your splash screen and then see a red *NA* in the notification area indicating that the current temperature has not been retrieved. If the MSN Weather service is available, you should see the current temperature for the Redmond, Washington, area in the notification area. (Be patient. Depending on the current Web service load, you might have to wait a few moments.) If you have to wait, you'll see that a little animated image displays while the data is coming back from the MSN server. You just have to enable it! When you double-click the temperature in the notification area, you should see detailed weather information, as shown in Figure 9-10. Right-click the temperature to see the context menu. When you have finished, exit the application.

Figure 9-10
The Weather Tracker application displaying weather data from a Web service

Working with the Options Dialog Box

Currently, the location is set to a particular value, and that really isn't our intent. Therefore, you will use the Options dialog box and let users search for the city they want to monitor. Once the location code is selected, it will be persisted to disk, and whenever users restart the application, it will be restored to the last location they specified. Remembering users' settings from one execution to another will provide them with a better experience.

You will use the error provider control to display appropriate text if no city is found.

The error provider control displays error information. For example, if the user enters invalid information in a text box, an error icon is displayed next to the control indicating that an error has occurred. By default, the error icon is a small red circle with an exclamation point. When the user clicks the error icon, an error description is displayed to explain what is wrong to the user. You can change how the error is presented. For example, you can use a different error icon, or you can make the error icon blink. Once a user addresses the error, you set the error description to an empty string to make the error icon disappear.

TO VALIDATE USER INPUT

1. Open the Options form in Design view.

2. In the Toolbox, drag an ErrorProvider control from the Components group to the form. The control appears in the component tray.

3. Name the control ErrorProviderCurrentLocation.

4. Double-click the OK button.

5. Add the following code to the *btnOk_Click* event handler:

```
UpdateCurrentInfo()
Me.DialogResult = Windows.Forms.DialogResult.OK
Me.Close()
```

6. You'll add some code to support when the user presses Enter while in the current city text box. You can see that you have to launch the search if there's something in the text

box. To capture the individual keys, you implement the *KeyDown* event handler. It fires as soon as the user presses a key. When the Enter key is pressed, you'll make a call to another MSN Web service to get the list of cities that have keywords in their metadata that matches your query. It's also here that you'll set the error provider to alert a user that the search didn't make any progress.

```
Private Sub txtCurrentCity_KeyDown(ByVal sender As System.Object, _
    ByVal e As System.Windows.Forms.KeyEventArgs) Handles _
    txtCurrentCity.KeyDown
    If (e.KeyCode = Keys.Enter) Then
        Me.Cursor = Cursors.WaitCursor
        UpdateListBox()
        If (lbPossibleCities.Items.Count = 0) Then
            ErrorProviderCurrentLocation.SetError(txtCurrentCity, _
                "No results for: " & txtCurrentCity.Text)
        Else
            ErrorProviderCurrentLocation.SetError(txtCurrentCity, "")
        End If
    End If
    Me.Cursor = Cursors.Default
End Sub
```

7. The *UpdateListBox* method says it all; this method will contact the MSN Weather service for the currently entered city, country, or other information and bind this list of *KeyValuePair* classes to the list box *Items* collection. The reason the *KeyValuePair* class has been used here is simple: you need *locationCode* to make the call to the MSN Web service, and you need the other one to display on the form as the current monitored location.

```
Private Sub UpdateListBox()
    Dim Locations As List(Of KeyValuePair(Of String, String))
    Dim myMSNWeather As New MSNWeatherData()
    Locations = myMSNWeather.GetLocations(txtCurrentCity.Text)
    lbPossibleCities.DataSource = Locations
    lbPossibleCities.DisplayMember = "Value"
    lbPossibleCities.ValueMember = "Key"
End Sub
```

1. In Options.vb, add the following *UpdateCurrentInfo* method:

```
Private Sub UpdateCurrentInfo()
    If ((txtCurrentCity.Text <> String.Empty) And _
        (lbPossibleCities.Items.Count <> 0)) Then
        If (Me.lbPossibleCities.SelectedValue.ToString() <>
            My.Settings.CurrentLocationCode) Then
            My.Settings.CurrentLocationCode = _
                Me.lbPossibleCities.SelectedValue.ToString()
            My.Settings.CurrentLocation = _
                Me.lbPossibleCities.SelectedItem.Value.ToString()
            Main.currentLocation = _
                Me.lbPossibleCities.SelectedItem.Value.ToString()
            Main.currentLocationCode = _
                Me.lbPossibleCities.SelectedValue.ToString()
        End If
    End If

    If rbCelsius.Checked = True Then
        My.Settings.CurrentUnit = "C"
        Main.currentUnit = "C"
    Else
        My.Settings.CurrentUnit = "F"
        Main.currentUnit = "F"
    End If

    My.Settings.Save()
    Main.UpdateWeather()
End Sub
```

The *UpdateCurrrentInfo* method saves the user's location code and location, as well as the unit selected to display the temperature, and stores those values with the application settings. It also calls the *UpdateWeather* method in the code for the Main form to update the weather data for the new location code. The *UpdateCurrentInfo* method is called when the user clicks OK in the Options dialog box.

Testing Weather Tracker Options

Now you will test the Options dialog box. Press F5 to run Weather Tracker. Once the splash screen disappears, right-click the icon in the notification area, and click Options. In the Options dialog box, test the location name. For example, try typing some garbage, and press Enter. In this case, you should get the error provider to the left of the text box, as shown in Figure 9-11, letting you know that there were no results for the search query you made!

When you have finished, type a valid location name, and click OK. Select the city from the list that matches the one you'd like to monitor. It is quite fast, and you should see weather data for the new location code.

You should be proud of yourself. You've developed an application with numerous complex features, and it works! The Weather Tracker application accomplishes the basic features established at the beginning of the chapter. There is plenty of room for enhancement. Now it's time to learn how to distribute Weather Tracker or another application.

Figure 9-11
The error provider control indicating an error

And Now, Just ClickOnce

The ClickOnce technology has been available since .NET Framework 2.0. It's a fantastic feature that lets you customize how your applications and tools get onto other people's machines. It's very easy—almost as easy as deploying Web applications, which often entails merely copying files onto a server. With ClickOnce, you, the developer, can distribute your application via a robust and reliable mechanism. You can deploy on Web servers, on file servers, or onto CDs/DVDs. In addition, you can add the .NET Framework to your distribution package along with SQL Server 2005 Express Edition if your application needs it. ClickOnce handles rollback and uninstall well, and it's a charm for pushing new updates. In this case, you'll deploy to a CD/DVD.

TO PACKAGE AND PUBLISH YOUR APPLICATION

1. To ensure that all the *.tif files representing the weather icons are included with the installation, make sure the *Build Action* property is set to *Content* for all the *.tif images in Solution Explorer. (This process was described earlier in the chapter.)

2. Rebuild the application by clicking Build Weather Tracker on the Build menu.

3. In Solution Explorer, right-click the Weather Tracker project, and select Properties to open the Project Designer.

4. Click the Publish tab. You should see a screen that looks like the one shown in Figure 9-12.

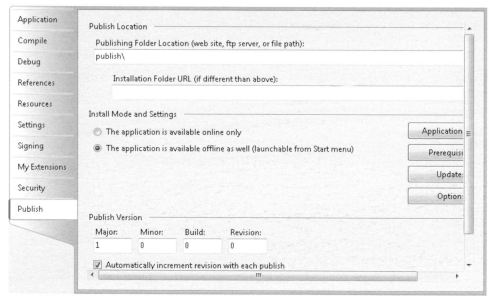

Figure 9-12
Publish tab in the Project Designer

5. Click the Application Files button to see the list of files that will be included in the installation. All the *.tif files (as well as the .exe and other files) should be listed. Click OK.

You now want to select the prerequisites for your application. When the installer runs on the user's machine, it will check for the presence of these items. If they are not present, the installer will by default download them from Microsoft.com or another source that you have configured.

6. Click the Prerequisites button. In the Prerequisites dialog box, select the .NET Framework 3.5 and Windows Installer 3.1 check boxes. Make sure the Download Prerequisites from the Component Vendor's Web Site option is selected. Click OK.

You can also set the Updates settings, which basically help you decide how your users will update their application and how frequently you want your application to automatically check for new updates. You won't do it here, but it's really trivial; take a look by clicking the Updates... button.

7. Click the Publish Wizard button.

The first page of the wizard appears, as shown in Figure 9-13, asking you to specify a location to publish the application.

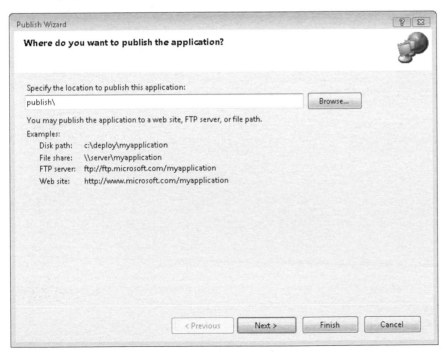

Figure 9-13
Publish Wizard's first page

8. Click the Browse button. In the Open Web Site dialog box, select File System on the left, and then select a location on your computer where you want to publish your application. I suggest you create a new folder named WeatherTracker. You can use the Create New Folder icon at the upper left to create a new folder. When finished, click the Open button, and then click Next.

9. On the next page, select how the user will install the application. It could be a Web site, a UNC share on a network, or a CD or DVD. Select the From a CD-ROM or DVD-ROM choice, and click Next.

10. The next page asks whether you want your application to look for updates every time it starts. Because you are deploying on a CD or DVD, you won't have your application check for updates. Select the default The Application Will Not Check for Updates choice, and click Next to continue.

11. Click Finish to publish your application.

After a few moments, setup files will be created at the folder location you selected earlier. To test the installation, double-click the Setup.exe file. During the installation, a shortcut will be added to the Programs menu. (To uninstall the application, use Control Panel.)

Once the installation works as expected, you can deploy your application by simply burning the installation files onto a CD or DVD.

ClickOnce has more features, but this short demonstration will get you started creating your own installations.

NOTE

Every time you publish your application, the published version number (not the application version number) will be incremented—that is, it will become version 1.0.0.0, 1.0.0.1, and so on.

NOTE

During the installation, if you get an error message that the application validation did not succeed or you receive another error message, try republishing your application and testing again.

In Summary...

Congratulations on getting this far! You've learned a lot, and I hope you've had some fun developing applications using Visual Basic 2008 Express Edition. If you like what you've learned (and I certainly hope so), then your education is just beginning. There's so much more to see and try. This book has provided a small sample of the types of applications you can create. My advice to you is to continue thinking of fun projects you can create! You'll be surprised at how much you can accomplish. In my opinion, developing an application is one the greatest feelings of accomplishment. People are proud of their applications, and you will be too!

If you happen to create an application that's useful to you, chances are it could be useful for others as well. In the end, you might be helping people by providing them with the fruits of your labor. You can also join development projects for fun and help others in the process while learning a great deal. Visit Codeplex (*http://www.codeplex.com/*) for a sample of cool project examples. Look also at Coding4Fun (*http://blogs.msdn.com/coding4fun/*), where you'll find plenty of interesting and new ways of using your new programming skills.

You can also visit my blog at *http://blogs.msdn.com/ppelland/*. I haven't updated my blog for a while because I've been busy writing this book, but my newest endeavor at Microsoft will enable me to blog about supercool technologies and talk about my new baby. It's still under wraps, but stay alert and come to my blog from time to time to see the news about the new project. Until then, happy developing!

Glossary

A

argument A variable that is passed to a subprogram

B

black box testing Functional testing of a computer program to ensure it performs correctly

breakpoint A pause or stopping place in a program, intentionally inserted to help with debugging

C

class The basic building block of object-oriented programming; it defines the fields, properties, methods, and events of an object

compiler A computer program that translates the instructions written in one computer language into output in another computer language; compilers translate source code into some type of machine language that can be executed by a computer

console application An application that is run from a command prompt with no Windows or Web interface

context-sensitive menu A menu that provides different choices to the user depending on when it is accessed

controls Components of a graphical user interface, such as text boxes or buttons

D

data member Data encapsulated within a class or an object

database A collection of data that is stored in files using a systematic structure

data binding An easy and transparent way to create a link between a control on a Windows form and a data source from your application

debugger A computer program used to find the defects in another program

DLL (Dynamic Link Library) A binary application library file format in Microsoft Windows

E

encapsulation Hides private methods of a class or object; ensures that an object cannot be changed

event A software message that indicates something has happened in the program

execution engine Development tool for executing programs

F

FCL (Framework Class Libraries) A set of code libraries for common programming tasks

H

hyperlink A reference in a hypertext document to another document or location

I

icon A small image or picture used to represent a program, file, or other object

IDE (Integrated Development Environment) Computer software tools that help developers write computer programs

inheritance The ability to create specialized types from existing objects that can share and extend the existing object's behavior without having to re-implement it.

instance A manifestation of a class

J

Jscript An Active Scripting Engine; the Microsoft version of JavaScript

L

Language Integrated Query (LINQ) Adds query capabilities to .NET programming languages (such as Visual Basic), enabling you to query data from a SQL Server database, XML, in-memory arrays and collections, ADO.NET datasets, or any other remote or local data source that supports LINQ

M

method Procedure or function; a piece of code associated with a class or object

Microsoft .NET A software development platform developed by Microsoft

O

override A class or object can replace a behavior it has inherited

P

Perl A programming language that supports both procedural and object-oriented programming

programming language A method for providing instructions to a computer

property A quality of an object

Python An object-oriented computer programming language

R

reference The address of the memory space used to store information about a variable

S

splash screen An image that appears on the screen while a program is loading; it provides information to the user about the loading process and disappears once the program is loaded

SQL Server 2005 Express Edition A version of SQL Server 2005 designed to help developers build applications by providing a powerful database that is also free and easy to use

string A sequence of characters or words

T

toolbar A row or section of clickable icons that activate different functions of a program

tooltip Short, context-sensitive information provided at the point where the mouse pointer is held

U

user interface (UI) The means by which users interact with a computer program

V

variable A structure that holds information temporarily for use later in a program

Visual Basic 2008 Express Edition A streamlined version of Visual Basic that provides hobbyists, students, and novices with an easy-to-use Windows programming and development tool

W

Windows application Computer software that provides various functions for the user, such as word processing, database queries, or spreadsheet calculations

Windows Presentation Foundation (WPF) Provides a framework for building applications for Windows Vista and blends together the application's user interface, documents, and media content

Index

Symbols

' (apostrophe), commenting code, 38

. (period), for opening IntelliSense, 64

A

About dialog box
  adding to Web browser application, 93–94
  attaching to Weather Tracker, 201
  creating, 199–201
  linking to Help menu, 94–96
abstraction, 211–12
Access databases, Microsoft, 163–64
actions. *See* methods
Add New Diagram, table relationships, 155–59
Add New Item, splash screens, 86
Add New Table, database tables, 153
Add Reference, 127
Add Table dialog, 177
Add to List Below drop-down list, menu items, 192–94
ADO.NET
  data binding and, 165
  Data Connection page, 166
  Data Sources window, 165–66, 168
  LINQ and, 164
  overview of, 163–64
  .xsd (XML schema document) and, 166–67
American Standard Code for Information Interchange (ASCII), 26

ANSI/ISO standards, 149
antispyware software
  installing Visual Basic 2008 Express and, 16
  updating, 22
antivirus software
  installing Visual Basic 2008 Express and, 16
  updating, 22
apostrophe ('), commenting code, 38
application creation, 25–46
  comparing application types, 26–27
  console applications, 31–39
  customizing IDE, 39–41
  overview of, 25
  starting Visual Basic 2008 Express IDE, 28–31
  Windows applications, 41–45
application deployment
  ClickOnce, 229
  packaging and publishing, 230–32
Application Files button, 230
applications
  debugging, 126
  references added to, 127–28
  types created with Visual Basic Express, 10
arguments. *See also* parameters
  defined, 235
  passing By Ref and By Val, 133
  passing data to methods, 54
arrays
  LINQ and, 164
  loops and, 135
  zero-basis of, 134

ASCII (American Standard Code for Information Interchange), 26
As keyword, IntelliSense and, 62
Assembly Information, 89–90, 201
AutoHide, enabling/disabling, 60

B

background performance
  supporting code for background tasks, 218–19
  of tasks, 215–18
  in Weather Tracker, 211
BackgroundWorker control, Windows Forms, 211, 215–18
Basic SQL, 149
binary data types, 160
binding navigators, 172. *See also* data binding
binding sources, 172. *See also* data binding
bitmap images, modifying splash screen images, 92
black box testing
  defined, 235
  testing own code, 98
breakpoints
  debugging tools/techniques, 128–29
  defined, 235
bugs. *See* debugging tools/techniques
build. *See* compile
Build Action property, 230
Build menu, 230
Button control, Windows Forms
  adding to Web browser application, 53

Click event connected to, 55–56
  description of, 76
buttons. *See also* Button control, Windows Forms
  adding to Web browser application, 106–07
  linking to Web browser functions, 105
  modifying navigation button behavior, 107–08
  renaming when adding, 106–07
By Ref, passing arguments, 133
By Val, passing arguments, 133

C

CarTracker
  creating with Visual Basic 2008 Express, 151–53
  data entry, 159–62
  dataset for, 166–72
  diagram, 150
  table relationships, 155–59
  tables, 153–55
Celsius to/from Fahrenheit conversion tool, 224
CharArray, 135
CheckBox control, Windows Forms, 77
classes
  ADO.NET, 163
  all classes deriving from *Object* class, 8
  common classes and methods in *My* namespace, 68–70
  defined, 235
  DLLs for grouping, 126
  examples of use of, 5–9

F

G

H

I

J

K

L